PEPYS
AT TABLE

PEPYS
AT TABLE

Seventeenth century recipes
for the modern cook

Christopher Driver and
Michelle Berriedale-Johnson

Book Club Associates
London

This edition published 1984 by
Book Club Associates

By arrangement with
Bell & Hyman Limited
Denmark House
37–39 Queen Elizabeth Street
London SE1 2QB

Designed by Paul Turner

ISBN 0 7135 2442 1

Typeset by Inforum Limited, Portsmouth
Printed and bound in Great Britain by
The Pitman Press Limited, Bath.

ACKNOWLEDGEMENTS

The updated recipes for Green Pea Soup (page 30), Steak Pie (page 48) and Gingerbread (page 102) first appeared in *Olde Englishe Recipes* by Michelle Berriedale-Johnson (Piatkus).

Illustrations from The Street Cries of London are reproduced by the courtesy of The Master and Fellows of Magdalene College. Cambridge. The Illustration from *The Queene-Like Closet or Rich Cabinet* (page 78) is reproduced by courtesy of The British Library. Other illustrations are adapted from *The Country Housewife and Lady' Director* by Richard Bradley, *A Display of Heraldry* (pub. 1678), a volume by Randle Holme (pub. 1905), *Hortus Santatis* (pub. 1485) and other seventeenth-century publications.

EPIGRAPH

'. . . and after greeting them, and some time spent in talk, dinner was brought up, one dish after another, but a dish at a time; but all so good, but above all things, the variety of wines, and excellent of their kind, I had for them, and all in so good order, that they were mightily pleased, and myself full of content at it; and endeed it was, of a dinner of about six or eight dishes, as noble as any man need to have I think – at least, all was done in the noblest manner that ever I had any, and I have rarely seen in my life better anywhere else – even at the Court. After dinner, my Lords to cards, and the rest of us sitting about them and talking, and looking on my books and pictures and my wife's drawings, which they commend mightily; and mighty merry all day long, with exceeding great content, and so till 7 at night; and so they took their leaves, it being dark and foul weather. Thus was this entertainment over, the best of its kind, and the fullest of honour and content to me that ever I had in my life, and shall not easily have so good again.

Diary IX 423–424

CONTENTS

INTRODUCTION

Samuel Pepys kept his famous Diary – a private document written in shorthand – for nearly ten years from the outset of his brilliant career at the Navy Office. It begins in 1660, when the twenty-six-year-old civil servant applauded the restoration of the monarchy he had hissed – as a Puritan schoolboy – at the execution of Charles I in 1649. The journal ends in 1669, shortly before the death of his wife Elizabeth at the age of twenty-nine.

Pepys was to rise further – and come near to falling from that great height – in his profession and vocation as Navy administrator. Office life is an important part of the Diary, but the nine volumes (plus Companion and Index) of the now-complete Latham and Matthews edition are mostly bought and read by general readers, not historians. Pepys is both life and literature, bundled into a single clever, passionate, pleasure-loving Londoner. His journal still reads more vividly than most novels. Was it yesterday or three centuries ago that he went to bed in a huff after rebuking his pretty, headstrong young wife for her untidiness? Is it our contemporary, or the trusted servant of Charles II, who took such pleasure in the combination of cream with brown bread (butter was at that time usually kept for cooking), and who voiced his repugnance at a friend's taste for very rare meat:

> It was an odd, strange thing to observe of Mr. Andrews what a fancy he hath to raw meat, that he eats it with no pleasure unless the blood run about his chops; which it did now, by a leg of mutton that was not above half-boiled; but it seems, at home all his meat is dressed so, and beef and all, and eats it so at nights also.

[In Pepys's time, the main meal of the day was taken before mid-day.]

By his own confession, good music and pretty (preferably compliant) women were his first loves. 'Music and women I cannot but give way to, whatever my business is.' But eating and drinking ran them close. Hence this little book, celebrating a neglected aspect of his age. It should enable twentieth-century hosts and hostesses to recreate on their own tables for social occasions the tastes that went with Marvell's verse, Purcell's music, Lely's pictures, Nell Gwyn's theatre, and Jeremy Taylor's sermons.

In the Diary we accompany Pepys into his food world: shop as well as kitchen, public tavern as well as domestic dining-room. Nevertheless, a dozen generations gone are a long time in the history of food and drink. Think how surprised we might be to meet in a friend's house the British bourgeois taste of thirty years ago, let alone three hundred: grey beef, tinned peas; no wine, no avocados. But it is at least possible to consult the recipe books of the time. Between 1650 and 1700, a new title of this kind was virtually an annual event in the London book trade – a trickle beside today's flood, but plenty compared with the drop-by-drop rate of Elizabethan publishing. On page 22 Michelle Berriedale-Johnson explains how to interpret such recipes for modern conditions, and each of the recipes that follow is given both in the original version (spelling included) and in a modern working adaptation.

But our intentions are not confined to recipe books.

There is much that even the scholarly editors of the Diary do not know about seventeenth-century eating, because the taste of food and drink cannot be preserved in museums like lutes or oil paintings or fine ladies' costumes. But there is also plenty – indeed, more and more – that we do know, or can plausibly imagine, from Pepys and other sources. Because it is no longer bad taste for Anglo-Saxon cultures to discuss the food people eat *now*, it is easier for historians and others to explore the food people ate *then*.

Pepys, in any case, ate and drank at an exceptionally interesting time. His century's changes in taste – changes then, as now, most obvious in polite London circles – scarcely affected the common people, or the sailors whose ships were victualled by Pepys's naval contractors. Material changes are another matter, and compared with Tudor times, most such changes were for the better. It is not part of the present purpose to discuss the incidence of actual hunger in seventeenth-century England. But if the poorest in the countryside still subsisted chiefly on bread and cheese and beer, and after a run of bad harvests had to survive on very little, the heavy English consumption of meat and fish which astonished visiting Frenchmen such as Misson and Sorbière was certainly not confined to the gentry. True, a rural labourer would think himself lucky with an occasional rabbit, fowl or pig. Everywhere in the winter, in the days before turnip crops, beasts had to be slaughtered and powdered (salted) for want of cattle feed. But salted or dried herrings were a popular breakfast,

8

large quantities of salt beef were loaded on to fighting ships, and in London, whose population was then about 400,000, a dish of neats' (calves') tongues at a tavern or a cut off the joint at a cookshop were never far away:

> Generally, four Spits, one over another, carry round each five or six Pieces of Butcher's Meat, Beef, Mutton, Veal, Pork and Lamb; you have what Quantity you please cut off, fat, lean, much or little done; with this, a little Salt and Mustard upon the Side of a Plate, a Bottle of Beer and a Roll; and there is your whole Feast.*

This account by the French traveller Misson relates to the 1680s. Many cookshops also baked to private commission when the dinner hour was over – once, the Pepyses sent a venison pasty to the baker through an unruly crowd, wondering 'whether any hurt would come to it'. The bread, too, whether baked on the premises or not, would have been wheaten, and as white as contemporary milling methods could make it, though Pepys's fellow-diarist John Evelyn conceded primacy to the French bakers in a paper he read to the Royal Society on the day Pepys was admitted in 1665 ('Panificium, or the several manners of making bread in France, etc., where by general consent the best bread is eaten'). Misson's 'Feast' described above would have cost him a shilling or two, roughly equivalent to a labourer's day wage at the time.

One puzzle about the diet of prosperous English people in the second half of the seventeenth century is its relative neglect of vegetables and salad stuffs, even after half a century of intensive development in the craft of gardening (much of it learnt from the Dutch). Evelyn, again, who wrote a whole book on the topic (*Acetaria, a Discourse of Sallets*) was far more enthusiastic than Pepys. The latter's frequent Diary references to food seldom mention greenstuffs, and his set-piece dinners often sound rather like the all-meat meals which travellers in the Périgord still sometimes encounter at old-fashioned country restaurants.

It is quite possible that Pepys ate roots and greens without caring about them enough to mention them. It is equally possible that he thought them bad for him. His digestion, though otherwise robust, was noticeably subject to wind and

---

* Misson de Valbourg, Henri. *M. Misson's Memoirs and Observations in his Travels over England* (1690), translated M. Ozell, 1719.

colic, and this was precisely the effect expected at the time from vegetables, not just from tubers such as Jerusalem artichokes and sweet potatoes (which preceded into English diet the types of potato now familiar). It was also considered inadvisable to eat vegetables and even much fruit raw.

However, in Pepys's time social cachet was attached to exotic fruit rather than to vegetables. It would not have been thought worthwhile at the time to despatch 'herbs' on long voyages from country to country – though the Elizabethan writer William Harrison refers to the arrival of 'very dangerous and hurtful verangenes' (aubergines, or as OED translates, 'brinjals') on a few noble tables. But for fruit, it is hard not to feel quite envious reading the Diary against the list of tree purchases made for the Woburn Abbey orchards at the same period. A Londoner in daily touch, as Pepys was, with the owners of great estates cannot have wanted for exotic produce throughout summer and autumn. One bill from Leonard Gurle's nursery in Whitechapel lists twelve varieties of peach, two of nectarine, eight of plum, eight of pear, three of cherry, three of apple, two of apricot, and one quince. Pepys could buy or pick cherries when he went down to visit the Kentish dockyards of Chatham and Rochester, or 'apricots for preserving' when he walked round Captain Cocke's estate at Greenwich. Fruit of this kind was a highly acceptable present, because – like the venison and other game that so many of Pepys's feasts depend upon – it did not normally reach the main London markets. The seventeenth-century Provost's privy recently investigated in the bowels of Oriel College, Oxford, revealed to Mark Robinson of the University Museum, after seed analysis, a similarly exotic diet, from Javanese peppers to Smyrna figs. But native raspberries and wild strawberries far outnumbered the rest.

The young Pepys liked shopping in those markets. The main one before the Great Fire of 1666 was not in the piazza of Covent Garden (which had only recently been licensed to the Earl of Bedford for this purpose) but at Leadenhall, 'where she and I, it being candle-light, bought meat for tomorrow, having ne'er a maid to do it; and I myself bought, while my wife was gone to another shop, a leg of beef, a good one, for sixpence, and my wife says is worth my money.' Pepys frequently 'picked up', as we would say, a rabbit or a barrel of oysters for supper at home, and on at least one occasion, arriving late with friends after Elizabeth and the servants had gone to bed, he dressed – that is, cooked – their fowl himself. Nor did his apparent neglect of vegetables detract from his pleasure in the first green peas of the year, and in April asparagus – 'So to the fishmonger's and bought a couple of lobsters, and over to the Spargus garden . . .' No mushrooms, though, in the Diary. English suspicion of fungi is of ancient origin, as William King also notices in his satirical *Journey to London* (1699):

> I desired to know what Mushrooms they had in the Market. I found but few, at which I was surpris'd, for I have all my Life been very Curious and inquisitive about this kind of Plant, but I was absolutely astonish'd to find, that as for Champignons, and Moriglio's, they were as great strangers to 'em as if they had been bred in Japan.

Pepys may not have shared Evelyn's love of sallets, but the Diary often echoes other movements of middle and upper class taste which sound oddly reminiscent of our own time: away from butcher's meat and towards poultry and game; from pickled herring to oysters and lobsters; from beer to wine, coffee, or chocolate. Some though not all of these changes were set off by a greater one, itself very familiar in our own century: the systematic influence of French cuisine on the ordering of the British table.

There has probably been no time since the Norman Conquest when French stylistic influences have been kept out of our kitchens altogether. Nor was France the only influence, according to William Harrison, writing in the high noon of Elizabethan patriotism:

> In number of dishes and change of meat the nobility of England (whose cooks are for the most part musical-headed Frenchmen and strangers) do most exceed, sith there is no day in manner that passeth over their heads wherein they have not only beef, mutton, veal, lamb, kid, pork, cony, capon, pig, or so many of these as the season yieldeth, but also some portion of the red and fallow deer, beside great variety of fish and wild fowl, and thereto sundry other delecates wherein the sweet hand of the seafaring Portugal is not wanting. . . *

But after the inward-turned Civil War and Commonwealth period continental influence expanded vigorously in Restoration London. Portuguese cooks and servants arrived in the

---

* William Harrison, *Description of England* (1577–87): extracted in Lothrop Withington (ed.), *Elizabethan England*, 1876

train of Charles II's ill-used Queen, the Infanta Catherine. Pepys and Evelyn both enjoyed an *oleo* (for which a recipe is given on page 60) at embassies and even private houses in London. Their descriptions are worth comparing. Pepys:

> We to the Mullberry-garden, where Sheres is to treat us with a Spanish *Oleo* by a cook of his acquaintance that is there, that was with my Lord in Spain. And without any other company, he did do it, and mighty nobly; and the *Oleo* was endeed a very noble dish, such as I never saw better, or any more of.†

Evelyn at 'the Portugal Ambassadors now newly come':

> The Entertainment was exceeding Civile, but besids a good *olio*, the dishes were trifling, hash'd and Condited after their way, not at all fit for an English stomac, which is for solid meate: There was yet good fowle, but roasted to Coale: nor were the sweetmeates good: I had much discourse with the Secretary, who seem'd an understanding person.‡

French cooking, then as now, was more admired than Iberian.

Charles II himself had spent much of his exile in Paris, consuming women at a scandalous rate but pausing to acquire other tastes – for the bright tone and undemanding airs of the 'vingt-quatre violons du Roy' as a change from the sober domestic sound of English viols, and possibly for sauces and ragouts in the style of la Varenne (see below). However, gourmandism was not one of the many indulgences popularly credited to Charles, and it was his sultry mistress Barbara Villiers (Lady Castlemayne) whose table the French Ambassador admired.

Pepys respected the shrewd brain the king had when he cared to use it, and often congratulated himself on the marks of royal favour he received. But he was no time-server. His own well-rooted qualities led him to despise most of Charles' courtiers both as men and as administrators, and his earthiness shows when he sits down to table in his own household. Entry after entry in the Diary suggests that he kept the tastes of

---

† Diary IX 509
‡ Diary (ed. E.S. De Beer 1959) p.677

his own family and childhood, eating what he enjoyed, not what fashion dictated. For instance:

> Home to dinner with my wife to a good hog's harslet, a piece of meat I love but have not eat of I think this seven year*

and

> Dined there with my wife upon a most excellent dish of tripes of my own directing, covered with mustard, as I have heretofore seen them done at my Lord Crews; of which I made a very great meal . . .†

These robust affections make his judgements sound more reliable as his horizons extend and finer or more elaborate dishes come his way.

Pepys's superb library (preserved in its entirety, bookcases and all, in his Cambridge college, Magdalene) contains a couple of little English cookery books, as well as a fifteenth-century household manuscript clearly bought – towards the end of his life – for antiquity rather than utility.‡ Neither book is mentioned in the Diary itself, and since Pepys not only often reports his book purchases but takes a close and combative interest in his wife's kitchen accounts, it is quite likely that both books were acquired after Elizabeth's death, perhaps to help Mary Skinner, his housekeeper and companion for the last thirty-three years of his life. (See page 116.)

In any case, these are but two books among many contenders for revival. In the pages that follow, we have attempted to match up some of the dishes eaten by Pepys during the 1660s with recipes current during his lifetime. We have allowed ourselves plenty of chronological latitude, in the light of the way cookery books are normally compiled, and of what happens to them after they are published. At least until the success of that startling twenty-five-year-old Isabella Beeton in mid-Victorian times, published cookery books normally reflected the practice of the author over a long working life, and word-for-word plagiarism from previous authors often augmented this conservative effect. Thus, the title page of Robert May's *Accomplisht Cook* (1660), a book much respected in

---

* Diary V 79
† Diary III 234
‡ G.A.J. Hodgett (ed.), *Stere htt well: mediaeval recipes and remedies from Samuel Pepys's Library* (Cambridge, 1972)

Pepys's time, refers to 'the fifty five Years Experience and Industry of Robert May, in his Attendance on several Persons of great Honour.' The author refers admiringly to his younger contemporary Sir Kenelme Digby, whose 'Closet' of recipes was published posthumously. (But Digby was the amateur, May the professional whose travels in France gave him no fewer than nine recipes for snails.)

Again, William Rabisha, author of *The Whole Body of Cookery Dissected* (1661), was 'Master Cook to many honourable Families before and since the wars began, both in this my Native Countrey and with Embassadors and other Nobles in certain forraign parts.' (Like all too many chefs, he was strange to the mischievous ways of printers: his disordered book opens with an apology for the misplacement of sections 'because the Author was absent in the Country.')

The books look back, then, when they are published but still have a long life ahead of them, re-issued if they are popular and handed down from cook to cook over a generation or two. (It is rare to find an old cookery book of any merit that is not stained and falling apart.) It is therefore fair to assume that almost any such book published within fifty years either side of the Diary decade is capable of casting some light on the kitchen economy Pepys knew as a young man. (See the check-list of books used on page 113.)

But one book published in this period explicitly looks forward rather than back, in an attempt to change the direction of English culinary practice, rather like the manuals of *nouvelle cuisine* which have reached the British book market in recent years. This is François de la Varenne's *Cuisinier françois* (1651), which was promptly 'Englished by J.D.G.' and first issued in London in 1653. It has a claim to be the first systematic cookery book on modern lines in the English language, and helps to explain why Pepys – a lover of neatness in all things – found the manner and order of French cuisine so seductive when he first encountered it. In this sense the structure of the book is more important than its contents, however impressed browsers must have been to find the '200 excellent Receits for the best sorts of Pottages, both in Lent and out of Lent', and what the foreword describes as 'several Sauces of Haut Goust, with dainty Ragousts, and Sweetmeats, as yet hardly known in this Land.' As Barbara Ketcham Wheaton explains, the system – based on a repertoire of bouillons, liaisons, and farces – is already modular, adaptable to a variety of materials, seasons, and conditions:

14

Favorite dishes from earlier centuries appear: venison pie and blancmange, for example, and a larded roast loin of veal, served with a vinegar, verjuice, and breadcrumb sauce, which Rabelais would have recognised. As is often the case when culinary change comes about recipes are not dropped immediately; rather, the repertory is enlarged to accommodate new inventions, while the old favorites linger on less prominently. . . But alongside these old stand-bys are new recipes that introduce a fresh array of textures and flavors. The replacement of porous bread trenchers by ceramic plates made it possible to serve both more liquid mixtures and firmer ones requiring the use of knife and fork.*

Pepys possessed two-pronged forks – a mediaeval invention from the Middle East, still considered Italian or otherwise advanced in England (in the 1660s, apparently, they were still not set at London Lord Mayors' banquets). He was also immensely proud of his store of plate (pewter and silver) for dinner parties. So he was prepared for the new era. And one thinks of Pepys again when Barbara Wheaton continues to discuss la Varenne:

A daube of mutton is made with herbs and orange peel, 'but very little, for fear of bitterness.' This moderation is characteristic of the new cookery: it is subtle but not bland. The long age of cinnamon and pepper had ended.

Well, not quite yet, remembering Lord Brouncker and Sir Edmund Pooly taking Pepys down into the hold of an India prize ship, 'and there did show me the greatest wealth lie in confusion that a man can see in the world – pepper scattered through every chink, you trod upon it; and in cloves and nutmegs, I walked above the knees – whole rooms full. . .'

Pepys's taste in food and drink evolves as his experience and resources grow, just as happens (sometimes) with our own contemporaries. He would have made an admirable inspector for a Restoration *Good Food Guide*; rather too ready, perhaps, to

---

For the publication dates of these and full title page details of these and other books, see A.W. Oxford, *English Cookery Books to 1850* and other standard culinary bibliographies.

---

* Barbara Ketcham Wheaton, *Savoring the Past: the French Kitchen & Table from 1300 to 1789*, (1983) pp.116–17

describe a dish of partridges or a chine of beef as 'the best I ever had' without further precision, but quite particular enough to notice that his cousin Thomas's venison pasty was 'palpable beef, which was not handsome,' or that his wife had injudiciously served him when they were alone 'a leg of mutton, the sawce of which being made sweet, I was angry at it and eat none, but only dined upon the Marrowbone that we had beside.' If the art of hospitality is compounded of generosity and taking pains (as it is), Pepys was a model host. Perhaps the most revealing of many descriptions belongs to the period when, except for a cook maid, he and Elizabeth had to do most things themselves. (Later, they could afford to employ a 'man-cook' for such occasions, and provide six or seven important dishes.) Pepys was already preoccupied on January 12th, 1663, the evening before the dinner party:

> So to my Lady Battens and sat with her a while, Sir W. Batten being gone out of towne; but I did it out of design to get some oranges for my feast tomorrow of her – which I did.
>
> So home, and find my wife's new gowne come home and she mightily pleased with it. But I appeared very angry that there was no more things got ready against tomorrow's feast, and in that passion sat up long and went discontented to bed.

The next day –

> So my poor wife rose by 5 a-clock in the morning, before day, and went to market and bought fowle and many other things for dinner – with which I was highly pleased. And the chine of beef was down also before 6 a-clock, and my own Jacke, of which I was doubtful, doth carry it very well. Things being put in order and the Cooke come, I went to the office, where we sat till noon; and then broke up and I home – whither by and by comes Dr. Clerke and his lady – his sister and a she-Cosen, and Mr. Pierce and his wife, which was all my guests.
>
> I had for them, after oysters – at first course, a hash of rabbits and lamb, and a rare chine of beef – next, a great dish of fowl, cost me about 30s, and a tart; and then fruit and cheese. My dinner was noble and enough. I had my house mighty clean and neat, my room below with a good fire in it – my dining-room above, and my chamber being made a withdrawing-chamber, and my wife's a good fire also. I find my new table very proper, and will hold nine or ten people

well, but eight with great room. After dinner, the women to Cards in my wife's chamber and the Doctor and Mr. Pierce in mine, because the dining-room smokes unless I keep a good charcole fire, which I was not then provided with. At night to supper; had a good sack-posset and cold meat and sent my guests away about 10 a-clock at night – both them and myself highly pleased with our management of this day . . . I believe this day's feast will cost me near 5 *l* [five pounds].*

Away from home, Pepys's choice of taverns for casual meals was clearly dictated as much by the presence of indulgent young women – and of private rooms to enjoy their company in – as by the quality of the food. But it was normal to find in such places a dish of anchovies or neats' tongues, and many places also offered a mid-day 'ordinary' – a set meal at a fixed price – on the lines of the cookshop described by M. Misson (above). Restaurants proper – as distinct from tavern set meals or take-away dishes from the *traiteur* – are not described until the 1760s in Paris, let alone London. But we owe an excellent account of the French restaurant in embryo to an impromptu decision made by Samuel and Elizabeth Pepys on a Sunday in May, 1667. Pepys obviously felt obliged to patch up a quarrel he had had with his wife about her desire to wear the fashionable 'white locks' instead of her own hair, and he must have known there would be trouble after a second disappointment, when their social call on Sir George Carteret found that gentleman already sitting down to his own meal:

I would not then go up; but back to the coach to my wife, and she and I homeward again; and in our way bethought ourselfs of going alone, she and I, to a French house to dinner, and so enquired out Monsieur Robins my periwig-maker, who keeps an ordinary, and in an ugly street in Covent-garden did find him at the door, and so we in; and in a moment almost have the table covered, and clean glasses, and all in the French manner, and a mess of potage first and then a couple of pigeons *a l'esteuvé*, and then a piece of *boeuf-a-la-mode*, all exceeding well seasoned and to our great liking; at least, it would have been anywhere else but in this bad street and in a periwig-maker's house; but to see the pleasant and ready attendance that we had, and all things

* Diary IV 13–14

17

so desirous to please and ingenious in the people, did take me mightily – our dinner cost us 6s.†

As often after French dinners, a walk then seemed desirable, and the Pepyses took coach to Islington and Hoxton, 'where we light and walked over the fields to Kingsland and back again, a walk I think I have not taken these twenty years but puts me in mind of my boy's time, when I boarded at Kingsland and used to shoot with my bow and arrows in these fields.'

The tone of that passage, boyhood reminiscence and all, matches agreeably the tone of countless letters which successive editors of *The Good Food Guide* have received from correspondents describing the merits of restaurants recently opened by Frenchmen for whom 'nothing was too much trouble.' Even at this date, 'the French manner' was distinctive in procedure and content alike. Until well on in the nineteenth century English dinners did not adopt the French sequential order of dishes, but were divided into two 'services' or groups of dishes. The first group was cleared away from the table before the second service – still mostly savoury but somewhat lighter, with an admixture of tarts and syllabubs or other sweet dishes – arrived in its turn.

Pepys had a tart, fruit, *and* cheese at his own feast. (Cheshire, Suffolk, and Dutch cheeses are all mentioned in the Diary, and that leaves out of account the Parmesan cheese that was buried in the garden for its own protection while the Great Fire was raging.) None of these things are mentioned at Monsieur Robin's Covent Garden ordinary, but at 3s a head this is hardly surprising, considering the price of them. The Twelfth Night cake 'cut in twenty pieces' for a dancing and singing party at Pepys's house in January 1668 'cost me near 20s of Jane's making.' Sugar was still very expensive.

As for the *potage*, stewed partridges, and *a la mode* beef, do the words 'exceeding well seasoned', which Pepys did not use lightly, indicate that even three centuries ago French cooks already expected to modulate the taste of their dishes well before they reached the table, while English diners more often

---

† Diary VIII 211

expected to add salt and perhaps mustard? At this stage, French cooks in London would have been recent immigrants, not yet adapted to English manners, and their numbers were augmented after 1685 by Protestant refugees, following Louis XIV's revocation of the Edict of Nantes.

Drinking with Pepys

With drink, as with food, Pepys's world has to be understood to be reproduced fairly and with moderate accuracy under twentieth-century conditions. As in our own time, and for similar reasons (travel, social change, and technical development) tastes were changing, both in the drinks and in the drinkers. For instance, a mere thirty years ago, the cheapest red wine on the British market was usually too harsh to be drunk without being mulled, hardly any women drank beer, and coffee, even instant, had yet to become a classless drink.

In the mid-seventeenth century, Royalists and Puritans alike enjoyed a wide choice of drinks, controlled chiefly by cost, tradition, and location. Some people still suppose that under Puritan influence half the population denied themselves alcohol and drank milk or water. That notion arises from the nineteenth-century Evangelical reaction against the social disorder induced, after Pepys's time, by cheap gin. (Dutch William and Dutch gin arrived together in the 1690s.) In the Diary period, spirits were expensive, wine was an upper middle class taste and extravagance, country cider was an acceptable substitute, and beers and ales (the latter unhopped) were the everyday, every age drinks, at about 2d a quart. This saved city-dwellers from the perils of the water. (Catherine of Braganza's retinue, used to pure mountain water conveyed to Lisbon by Roman aqueducts, found London well-water disgusting.) Brewing was of course mostly local and small-scale. One day, Pepys happens to mention changing his brewer, though on occasion he also tasted ales of repute from further afield, such as Margate or Northdown.

It was a long time before the newer non-alcoholic drinks made any serious difference to this pattern. In the 1660s, coffee and coffee houses were a recent development, introduced to London via Oxford by an enterprising Jew. Coffee soon became an indispensable and relatively inexpensive habit among the intelligentsia. Chocolate was dearer, and more ladylike perhaps, than beer or coffee, and more nourishing too, since it was often drunk with sack (white wine) and egg mixed

19

in, and retained the cocoa butter which is subtracted from today's drinking chocolate. Tea, which Pepys first tasted in 1660, arrived from China through Holland and cost £2 a pound – a sum roughly equivalent to thirty tavern dinners. Fruit juices were a novelty, buttermilk at a 'whey-house' a fad of Pepys's shared by many others, and milk itself also an option, though (rightly) considered unsafe by some.

In the 1980s – thanks more to activist consumers than to the brewing combines – undoctored local beers and even ciders are to be found here and there on the market. The persevering might consider building their Pepys parties round these mostly native drinks. Wine, though still grown on a few English estates in the Diary period, was mostly imported in hogshead from various European sources, and decanted into bottles only for serving at table. The invention of the cork, permitting long-term storage in bottles, was a vinous technical development that still lay just over the horizon in 1660. Wine was therefore drunk young, and the potential excellence of particular growths could hardly be appreciated, although Pepys, predictably, is the first English author to name the chateau whose claret he had drunk: 'Ho Bryan'.

Modern hosts would therefore be wasting their money by offering well-aged Chateau Haut Brion at Pepysian occasions. But their care for their own cellars is unlikely to exceed his. By 1666, Pepys was 'taking notice to what a condition it hath pleased God to bring me, that at this time I have two tierces of claret – two quarter-cask of canary, and a smaller vessel of sack – a vessel of tent [that is, Spanish red wine, *tinto*], another of Malaga, and another of white wine, all in my wine-cellar together – which I believe none of my friends of my name now alive ever had of his own at one time.' Earlier, he had admired – with a charming and typical comparison – the cellar kept by a pioneer connoisseur, Thomas Povey, 'where upon several shelves there stood bottles of all sorts of wine, new and old, with labells pasted upon each bottle, and in that order and plenty as I never saw books in a bookseller's shop.'

Generic German wines would also be appropriate for a Pepys party, for Rhenish wine houses were favourite resorts of his, both before and after he vowed to give up the excessive drinking which upset both his stomach and his head in the first flush of Restoration euphoria and professional advancement. At the close of the century William King (quoted above, page 11) mentions Volnay and Condrieu among other French wines, but he had not necessarily tasted them. Woburn, at this time, was importing Chablis, 'Provence claret' whatever that was, and also Navarre wine – properly, Jurançon. (The Duke of York commended that wine to Pepys, along with the recipe for the Spanish Ambassador's favourite all-purpose sauce.) Moreover, and still within the Diary period, the Earl of Bedford's cellar took in a more significant harbinger of the British aristocracy's future drinking: four dozen *bottles* of Sillery Champagne, price £6.

Other wine names can be traced for the period, through the Index to the Diary and through other sources. But to save people's heads at parties, it is worth pointing out that 'sherris-sack' is not sherry as we understand the word, because both the *flor* and the fortification were later Jerez developments. White Rioja or, if the sherry taste is desired, the unfortified Montilla may approximate to the 'sack' Pepys drank. He had to pay more for the softer, dearer Malaga (later a favourite with the Victorians in its sweet form, and still obtainable from specialist wine merchants). Other raisiny dessert wines are also permissible, though in Pepys's time they were more often imported from Italy and the Levant than from France and Spain. One or two recipes for spiced or mulled treatments of wines and ales appear on page 75.

Christopher Driver 1984

21

COOKERY INTRODUCTION

In culinary terms, as in political, the seventeenth century saw the dawn of the modern world. Not only was it the first century in which cookery books were widely bought and used, by the educated classes at least; it was also the first in which an active general interest was taken in the propagation of new food stuffs and the adoption of new culinary ideas.

By the early 1600s English horticulturalists such as the Tradescants, father and son, were importing strange and exciting fruits and vegetables from the New World and cultivating them, more or less successfully, at home. By the 1660s (Pepys's time) the revolutionary French haute cuisine was seeping across the channel, greatly encouraged by Charles II's court which had spent the years of its exile soaking up the new culinary forms at the court of Louis XIV.

In domestic English kitchens, whose mistresses were normally now literate, change was also afoot. Mediaeval recipes, where they existed at all, were either extremely brief, leaving nearly everything to the experience and personal preference of the cook, or else so complicated as to be incomprehensible to all but culinary historians. Late seventeenth-century recipes are sufficiently 'modern' for a twentieth-century cook to be able to understand, at first reading, how the dish should be prepared.

However the very fact that those recipes can be read and understood presents its own problems. Raw materials do not always equate with our own in character, size or quality; seventeenth-century tastes, although closer to our own than the Elizabethans', are not our own, so flavourings need to be tested before being adopted wholesale. Still, one of the fascinations of late Stuart and early Georgian cookery is how exactly many of the recipes can be followed to produce bizarre, yet very effective results – see Hannah Wolley's Bacon Tart on page 63.

However, seventeenth-century recipes, like their predecessors, were not intended to be rigidly adhered to; they were ideas which the writer had inherited, purloined or sometimes invented, and expected other cooks to adapt in their turn. In modernising the recipes for this book I have tried to follow the originals as closely as possible, except where the flavour was likely to be so foreign to modern taste as to be totally unacceptable – for example, Gervase Markham's Herring pie.

In a true seventeenth-century spirit of enquiry, more enter-prising cooks might like to try their own adaptations. I am therefore listing a few basic differences between our own ingredients and those that Joan Cromwell or Hannah Wolley might have used.

Meat

An efficient means of feeding more than a small nucleus of farm animals through the winter months was not fully developed till the eighteenth century. As a result stock breed-ing as we know it scarcely existed. The so-called domestic or farm animals were still virtually wild, or, in culinary terms, tough and sinewy. To combat toughness meat was hung to mature it and break down the fibres; heavily spiced or pickled to tenderise it, or cooked very long and slowly. Twentieth-century meat is of much better quality, in terms of texture at least, so needs less maturing, spicing and cooking.

Since there was not enough fodder to keep them all alive, the majority of the animals were killed during the period from September to Christmas and pickled, soused, smoked or dried to preserve their flesh as long as possible. These methods of preservation were effective but left a strong flavour of their own which in turn needed to be counteracted by heavy spicing and flavouring. Now that freezers do our preserving for us without imparting taste we do not need such heavy disguise for our meat.

But whether the meat was spiced or newly killed there were no refrigerators to prolong its freshness. In this respect the Pepyses were lucky – they lived in London which was well supplied with fresh and reasonably good quality meats, but even they had to take care. On more than one occasion Pepys complains about bad venison in a pasty. As a safeguard, meats were very thoroughly cooked or served, as they had been in the middle ages, with a sweet, spicy or fruity sauce. The natural antiseptic in the spices and acid fruits helped to counteract any 'poisins' in the meat. Since we seldom need worry about freshness in our meat we can reduce the length of cooking and the strength of the sweet or spicy sauces.

Fish

Transport was slow and limited, so unless you lived close to a source of fresh fish (the sea, a river, inland lake or fish ponds)

23

you were unlikely to eat fish at all unless it were pickled or dried – hence Markham's recipe was for pickled herring which would have been available all year round. Shellfish was popular as most species could be kept alive for several days in tanks on journeys inland. Shellfish were also easily obtainable and therefore relatively cheap – hence the number of recipes for lobsters and oysters which, for the sake of modern pockets, I have transposed to prawns and mussels.

Vegetables

Despite the enthusiasm for cultivating imported fruits and vegetables little had been done to improve native stocks. Thus most root vegetables were still relatively wild – long, thin, hairy and a great deal tougher than our own. To make them palatable, and more digestible, they were cooked far longer than we would find necessary and 'seasoned' with enormous quantities of butter to improve the texture – see the 'Sweet potato pudding' on page 82. Moreover all vegetables and fruits were seasonal – which is why books of the period have as many or more recipes for preserving or candying fruits and vegetables as they do for 'straight' cooking. The seventeenth-century housewife had to be much better organised than her twentieth-century counterpart. If she failed to preserve her fruits or vegetables when they were in season there was no corner shop to rescue her. The family would just have to do without until the next year.

Dairy Produce

Dairy produce was also seasonal – cows had not yet been trained to give milk all year round. This meant that cows' milk was not always available and when it was it varied in quality. As for cream: in the spring when the grass was lush and new cream would be as thick and rich as modern double or heavy cream; in the late autumn or early winter no richer than modern single or coffee cream. Similarly good cheese could only be made in the spring or early autumn when the milk was fat and rich. Butter was made year round but could only be preserved, and then not very effectively, by heavy salting. As a result it was always strong tasting and often rancid. It was seldom eaten raw although used extensively for cooking; it was thought to help digestion.

Eggs were plentiful but much smaller than those from our overdeveloped battery hens.

24

Flour

The type of flour you used for your daily bread depended on where you lived. In the north, oats formed the staple; in the midlands and eastern counties much rye was grown and so on.

Even when white flour is called for this does not mean 'white' in our sense, but fine wholemeal flour. Only when the roller mill was invented in the nineteenth century did it become possible to crush the wheat germ and release the chalky white and longlasting 'flour' from within. Stone milling merely produced various gradations of whole germ flour from which the impurities were removed by repeated sievings or 'boultings' through coarse linen cloth.

Pastry

Until the seventeenth century most pastry had been hot water crust; a robust pastry which worked well as a container, its main purpose in mediaeval cookery. However, by Pepys's time cold fat was being used to make a shorter and crisper paste, both shortcrust and puff. Where pastry is required in the following recipes use a shortcrust paste made with wholemeal flour and half the flour's weight in butter, or mixed butter and lard.

Sauces and Gravies

Reference is often made in the original recipes to a 'good brown gravy'. This normally refers to a rich meat stock known as a cullis which was the basis of most sauces but since it required half a farmyard to achieve it is both expensive and impractical to make. The juices from a roast or a good espagnole sauce make a quite acceptable substitute.

Cooking Equipment

By the mid-seventeenth century most kitchens did at least have a cooking hob – usually brick built with an open fire beneath – and some kind of an oven. However, both of these relied on an open wood fire which made it extremely difficult to guarantee any constant heat – or indeed any specific heat at all! You will therefore seldom get any indication in old recipes of the temperature needed to cook a certain dish or much idea of how long it should be cooked. Where such indications are given they are usually for longer times than the greater accuracy of our own equipment require.

GRAVYSOOP

1669 March 15th

'Up and by water with W. Hewer to the Temple; and
thence to the Chapel of Rolles . . . and so spent the
whole morning with W. Hewer, he taking little notes
in short-hand, while I hired a clerk there to read to me
about twelve or more several rolls which I did call
for. . . At noon they shut up, and W. Hewer and I did
walk to the Cocke at the end of Suffolke-street, where
I never was, a great ordinary, mightily cried up, and
there bespoke a pullet; which while dressing, he and I
walked into St. James' park, and thence back and
dined very handsome, with a good Soup and a pullet
for 4s-6d the whole.'

A successful eating house like the Cocke would no doubt have
made good use of all its leftovers by turning them into soups
they could sell the following day. Pepys does not specify what
kind he and Will Hewer were given but it could have been a
'gravysoop' like the one Ann Blencowe tells us she got from the
Sergeant's Inn cook. On the other hand the cook might have
used the bones from all those 'pullets' as the base for a white
malgre or maigre soup as suggested by Patrick Lamb – though
for 4s-6d you would be unlikely to have got all those poached
eggs. . .

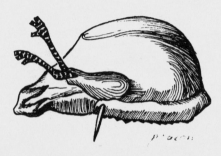

TO MAKE GRAVYSOOP

The Receipt Book of Mrs. Ann Blencowe 1694

'Have a good strong broth made of a Legg of beef and seson'd with time and Cloves and mace, and when 'tis well boyld that you think it will jelly when 'tis cold, strain it off ye broth from ye meat. Then put your broth into a pot that you designed to make your soop in and have in readiness these soop herbs viz; some Sallery and judiss and spinidge. Clean them and chop them small and stew them well in a stew pan over a clear fire. Then put them into your broth and let them boyl gently and some Oxes pallets and let them be boyl'd very tender and cut them in very small slices. Then put them into your soop, and season it with peper and salt and Nutmeg to your pallet, and dish it up with a Roasted duck or fowl in ye middle and dry some french bread and break it into your soop. So serve it.'

Recipe Serves 6

12 small slices French bread
1½ ozs /40 g beef dripping
4 ozs /100 g finely chopped onion
2 stalks of celery, very finely chopped
4 ozs/100 g fresh spinach, chopped
¼ teaspoon ground cloves
2½ pts /1½ litres good homemade beef stock
4 ozs /100 g cooked tongue, cut in matchsticks
salt and pepper

Dry the slices of bread in a cool oven.
Melt the fat in a saucepan, add the onions and celery and fry gently until soft but not coloured. Add the spinach, cloves and stock, bring to the boil and simmer 15 minutes. Add the tongue and season to taste with salt and pepper.
Serve with the French bread floated on the top.

27

WHITE MALGRE SOUP

TO MAKE A WHITE MALGRE SOUP

Patrick Lamb *Royal Cookery* 1710

'Take six heads of Endive, a handful of sorrel, a little chervil, parsley and onion minced small, and herbs minced also, being very clean washed, stew them down in a saucepan with a quarter of a pound of butter for a quarter of an hour; then add 2 quarts of clear broth or boiling water, if the master will have no broth. Your herbs being boiled tender, skim the fat off and thicken your herbs with the yolks of 10 to 12 eggs, according to the bigness of your dish; scrape a nutmeg and the juice of half a lemon, if your sorrel is not sharp enough. Your bread being soaked in your dish as aforesaid, put in the middle of a French roll fryed. Let your garnishing be 8 to 10 poached eggs and fryed bread betwixt them on the outside of your Rim on the Dish, cut in small dice; you may put a poached egg on top of your French roll in the middle of your soupe being just thickened up with eggs hot over the fire. Set off your dish on the table, before you fill it up, because your Eggs may not curdle in your Soupe. So serve it.'

Recipe   Serves 4

1 head – approx 4 ozs /100 g chicory (white endive)
1 oz /25 g spinach or sorrel
2 large sprigs of parsley or chervil or both
1 small onion
1 oz /25 g butter
a sprig each of rosemary, thyme and basil or oregano
2 pints /1.2 litres clear chicken stock or a mixture of stock and water or
*   wine (white) and water*
3 egg yolks
pinch of nutmeg
juice 1 lemon
salt and pepper
4 whole eggs
4 slices French bread (optional)

Chop the chicory, spinach or sorrel, parsley or chervil and onion fairly small and put them in a pan with the butter. Chop the herbs, add them and cook them gently for 15 minutes. Add the liquid, bring to the boil and simmer for a further 15 minutes. Beat together the egg yolks, nutmeg, lemon juice and some salt and pepper. Remove the soup from the heat, add a ladleful to the egg yolk mixture, mix well and return it to the pan. Heat gently to thicken without allowing it to boil. Just before serving, poach the four whole eggs till just set. Pour the hot soup into four bowls and float a poached egg in each.

If you wish to use the bread, toast the slices of French bread, top each with a poached egg and float the whole thing on the soup as you serve it.

GREEN PEA SOUP

Although dried peas frequently appeared on everyone's table, especially in the winter, there are plenty of recipes for fresh pea soup – most of which are excellent. Pepys does not specify whether the Cocke's soup was dried or fresh, although April would have been somewhat early for fresh peas. Mrs. Blencowe's recipe also refers only to 'peas' but it is so good with fresh peas that I am assuming that is what she had in mind. . . .

TO MAKE PEAS SOOPE

The Receipt Book of Mrs. Ann Blencowe 1694

'Take about two Quarts of peas and boyl them down till they are thick; then put to them a leeke and a little slice of bacon and a little bunch of sweet herbs and let them boyl till they are broke. Then work them with ye back of a ladle thro a coarse hair sieve; then take about 3 pints of your peas and mix with about 3 quarts of very strong broth and work them very well together. Then sett them over a Stove and let them boyl very easily. Then as for your herbs, take out the quantity of a gallon of soope; take a large handfull of spinage and one third of sorrill and one cabbage, Lettice and a little Charvell and Cresses and a head or

two of sallery and Indive, and ye
heart of a Savoy and a little mint,
but mince your mint very small if it
be green, but if it be dry, then drie it
before ye fire to powder and sift it
through a sieve, and mince ye herbs
with one leeke very small and put
them into a brass dish or saspan with
half a pound of butter and let ym
stove till they begin to be tender.
Then put to them a quart of good
gravy or strong broth but gravy is

best, and when you have mix't it well then putt it into ye pott
to ye pease and a little beaten cloves and mace. So let it stove
about half an hour, then have a french roll, either dry'd in the
oven or toasted by ye fire, in thin slices, then season ye soope
to your palate and so serve it up. If you please you may put
forced meat balls into it, or any other thing as pallattes and
sweetbreads or Combs.'

Recipe   Serves 6

1 lb / 450 g fresh or frozen green peas
1 leek, finely sliced
1 clove garlic crushed
1½ oz / 40 g bacon, diced
3 ozs / 75 g butter
2 pints /1.2 litres ham stock
1 oz / 25 g fresh spinach
1½ ozs / 40 g white cabbage, finely sliced
¼ lettuce, finely chopped
small handful of parsley, finely chopped
1 stalk celery, finely chopped
½ carton of mustard and cress
1 teaspoon dried or fresh (chopped) mint
salt, pepper and a pinch of mace

Put the peas, leeks, garlic and diced bacon into a saucepan
with half the butter. Fry gently till the vegetables are softened
but not coloured. Add the stock. Bring to the boil and simmer
for 20 minutes. Liquidise or purée.
Meanwhile melt the rest of the butter in another pan and
sweat the spinach, cabbage, lettuce, parsley, celery, mustard
and cress and the mint till soft. Add to the puréed peas and
season with salt, pepper and mace. Reheat to serve.

PARMESAN AND EGGS

1666 September 4th

'. . . the fire coming on in that narrow street, on both sides, with infinite fury. Sir W. Batten . . . did dig a pit in the garden . . . and I took the opportunity of laying all the papers of my office that I could not otherwise dispose of. And in the evening Sir W. Penn and I did dig another and put our wine in it, and I my parmazan cheese as well as my wine and some other things.'

Pepys and Elizabeth were lucky; their house, unlike so many others, escaped the ravages of the Great Fire. As for Pepys's 'parmazan cheese' – maybe, after its experiences, it would have been better grated and baked as in Giles Rose's recipe. . . .

EGGS AND CHEESE

Giles Rose *A perfect School of Instruction for the Officers of the Mouth* 1682

'Beat a dozen egg with half a pound of Milan cheese grated, season it with pepper and bake it in a patty pan, with clarified butter, over a soft Fire and when it is baked serve it away without anything about it.'

Recipe   Serves 4

4 eggs
6 ozs /160 g freshly grated Parmesan cheese
black pepper
1 oz / 25 g butter

Whisk the eggs lightly in a bowl, then add the grated cheese and season well with black pepper.

Melt the butter in the bottom of a 6 inch/15 cm flan dish, pour in the egg mixture and bake in a moderately cool oven (325°F/160°C/ Gas Mark 3) for 20 minutes or till it is slightly risen and browned. Eat immediately with fresh brown bread and butter.

BUTTERED EGGS WITH ANCHOVIES

1663 April 4th

'. . . which I having done, I returned home to dinner.

Whither by and by come Roger Pepys, Mrs. Turner, her daughter, Joyce Norton and a young lady, a daughter of Collonell Cockes – my uncle Wight – his wife and Mrs. Anne Wight – this being my feast, in lieu of what I should have had a few days ago, for my cutting of the Stone, for which the Lord make me truly thankful.

Very merry before, at, and after dinner, and the more for that my dinner was great and most neatly dressed by our own only mayde. We had a Fricasse of rabbets and chicken – a leg of mutton boiled – three carps in a dish – a great dish of a side of lamb – a dish roasted pigeons – a dish of four lobsters – three tarts – a Lampry pie, a most rare pie – a dish of anchoves – good wine of several sorts; and all things mighty noble and to my great content.'

Pepys and Elizabeth's friends could always be guaranteed an excellent dinner at Pepys's annual celebration of his operation. Although one cannot but sympathise with the 'only mayde' who did not have the help of a temporary cook as on subsequent occasions. I wonder if she still had energy enough left to 'butter' her 'dish of Anchoves' as in this recipe from *The Family Dictionary* of 1695.

BUTTERED EGGS WITH ANCHOVES

The Family Dictionary 1695

'Break twenty eggs into your Butter in a Dish and set them on Coals, take six Anchoves, and dissolve them in six spoonfuls of White-wine, and put them to your Eggs, and having one handful of Pistaches beaten small in a Mortar, put them into your Eggs with a quarter of a Pint of Mutton Gravy: If you please you may leave out your White-wine and dissolve your Anchoves in Mutton-Gravy: let not your eggs be too stiff; then having a Dish full of Toasts, cut into large Sippets, lay your eggs by spoonfuls on the Toasts, or else dish them otherways with Toasts about them, on the Brims of the Dish.'

Recipe   Serves 6

6 large fillets of tinned anchovies
3 tablespoons white wine
12 eggs
1½ ozs / 40 g pistachio nuts, finely chopped
4 tablespoons of good brown juice from a roast or casserole
1 oz / 25 g butter
6 slices wholemeal bread, toasted

Mash the anchovies in the white wine. Lightly whisk the eggs in a bowl, then add the anchovies and wine, nuts and gravy. Melt the butter in a pan, add the egg mixture and cook gently as for scrambled eggs. Serve the eggs either on or with freshly toasted brown bread and a little freshly ground black pepper.

SPINACH TANZY

1662 March 26th

'Up early – this being, by God's great blessing, the fourth solemne day of my cutting for the stone this day four year. . . . At noon came my good guest Madam Turner, The [Theophila] and Cosen Norton, and a gentleman, one Mr. Lewin of the King's life-guard. . . . I had a pretty dinner for them – *viz*: a brace of stewed Carps, six roasted chicken, and a Jowle of salmon hot, for the first course – a Tanzy and two neats' tongues and cheese the second. And we were very merry all the afternoon, talking and singing and piping on the Flagelette.'

The tanzy must have almost got lost in all the good fare that Pepys served for his annual celebration of the day in 1655 when he was successfully 'cut for the stone'. He knew his luck; most patients died. William Rabisha's Tanzie is excellent but rich. If you prefer a firmer and less filling texture, 'deminish' the cream to 10 fl oz/300 ml and the extra egg yolks to three.

TANZIE OF SPINNAGE

William Rabisha *The Whole Body of Cookery Dissected* 1661

'Take a pint of Cream, a handful of
grated bread, fourteen eggs, cast
away the whites of six, season it with
a grated Nutmeg, and sugar, and
green it with the juice of Spinnage;
so bring it into a body, in a skillet,
and fry it. This will be a very tender
Tanzie; but if you intent to cut it
according to the vulgar way, you
must add the other whites of eggs,
else deminish in your Cream; dish it
up, scruise (sic) on the juice of a
Lemmon, and garnish it with
guartered Oranges, then scrape on
Sugar. After this way and manner
aforesaid, have I made Tanzies of
Wallnut-tree buds in Lent, and of
Pine-apples and Pistaches, at other
seasons.'

Recipe   Serves 6

12 ozs / 350 g fresh spinach chopped small
5 fl oz /150 ml water
2 ozs / 50 g butter
6 egg yolks plus 6 whole eggs
3 ozs / 75 g brown breadcrumbs
½ teaspoon nutmeg
sea salt and black pepper
15 fl oz / 450 ml whipping cream
1 oz / 25 g butter

Cook the spinach gently in the water for 15 mins. Drain off
any water that is left, add the butter and continue to cook for
a further 15 minutes.
Whisk together the eggs, egg yolks, breadcrumbs, seasonings
and cream. Add the spinach.
Heat the remaining butter till sizzling in a large, wide pan,
pour in the mixture and cook as for an omelette for 2 minutes.
Then put the pan under a very hot grill to brown and cook
the top. Alternatively, cook six individual omelettes. Serve
immediately.

STEWED PRAWNS OR SHRIMPS

No doubt the 'Codd and prawnes' that 'Sir Wms.', Sir George and Pepys took with them for their journey were cold – how much better off they would have been if they could have had some of Robert May's good warming 'stewed prawns' to keep out all that wind and rain.

TO STEW PRAWNS, SHRIMP AND CRAYFISH

Robert May *The Accomplisht Cook* 1660

'Being boiled and picked stew them
in white wine, sweet butter, nutmeg
and salt, dish them in scallop shells
and run over them over with beaten
butter and juyce of orange or lemon.'

Recipe   Serves 4

2 ozs / 50 g butter
5 fl oz / 150 ml white wine
½ teaspoon each of grated nutmeg and sea salt
1 lb / 450 g prawns or shrimps, shelled
juice of 2 oranges

Melt the butter in a pan with the wine, nutmeg and salt; add
the fish and simmer gently for 15 minutes. Add the orange
juice and adjust the seasoning to taste. You could serve the
prawns with Sir Kenelme Digby's rice page 79.

HERRING PIE

Ling is a white fish caught mainly in the North Sea. Because
it kept so well dried and salted it was much used, though not
on the whole much loved, throughout the winter months.
Our nearest equivalent is salt cod, but this has a very distinctive flavour and except as an experiment, most people avoid
it!

Gervase Markham would most probably have used pickled
herrings in his pie. That meant he could make it at any time
of the year, just by dipping into his herring barrel. Since the
flavour is strong for twentieth-century palates the recipe has
been adapted to suit fresh herrings too.

It is amusing to note that Pepys never allowed his amours
or conscience to interfere with his appetite.

AN HERRING PIE

Gervase Markham *The English Hus-wife* 1615

'Take white pickled herrings, boil them a little, remove the skin, keep the backs only and remove the bones. Put them in a pastry casing with some raisins, some sliced winter pears or quince sliced very fine, sugar, cinnamon, sliced dates, sweet butter. Cover and leave a vent at the top. Bake. Take claret, a little verjuice, sugar, cinnamon, and sweet butter. Boil them together and then pour them through the vent-hole, shake the pie a little and put it back into the oven for a few minutes. Candy the pastry lid with sugar and water and glaze it in the oven.'

Recipe   Serves 6

6 fresh or pickled herrings
8 ozs / 225 g wholemeal pastry
1½ ozs / 40 g plump raisins
1½ ozs / 40 g dates, stoned and sliced lengthways
3 fresh pears, peeled, cored and sliced
1½ ozs / 40 g butter
6 fl oz /180 ml red wine
3 fl oz / 90 ml wine vinegar
salt and pepper to taste and a pinch of cinnamon

Depending on whether you want a bland flavour to your pie or the sharp tang of the original, simmer the fresh herrings in boiling water then bone and skin them, or, drain and fillet the pickled herrings. Roll out two-thirds of the pastry and line an 8 inch/20 cm flan dish. Break up the herring and lay a layer of fish in the bottom of the pie. Sprinkle the raisins and dates over the fish, then the sliced pear and top with the rest of the fish. Roll out the rest of the pastry and cover the pie. Decorate the lid but leave a vent hole in the middle. Cook the pie in a moderate oven (375°F/180°C/Gas Mark 5) for 30 minutes. Meanwhile, gently simmer the butter, wine, vinegar and seasonings. Remove the pie, pour the juices through the vent hole, and return the pie to the oven for a further 15 minutes. Serve warm.

TO COOK TROUT

'Bad and mean' Hungerford may have been but at least it was on the river which provided it with a constant supply of fresh fish – a luxury not easily obtained at any distance from the coast. The recipe below comes from one of the only two cookery books in Pepys's own library although both were probably used after Elizabeth's death by Mary Skinner, Pepys's housekeeper and companion in his later years.

TO COOK MULLET, TENCH, TROUT OR CARP

The Gentlewoman's Delight in Cookery

'Take the fish well drawed, supplying the vacancy of the Belly with sweet herbs: boil them in water a little seasoned with Salt; and when enough, take butter, Grated bread, the Juyce of Orange, Cinnamon with Currans; make them into a Sawce with Herbs, and serve them up with Green Garnish.'

42

Recipe Serves 4

4 fresh trout, cleaned
4 sprigs each of rosemary, fennel tops, parsley and marjoram
10 fl oz / 300 ml water
pinch sea salt
4 slices orange
1 oz / 25 g butter
1 oz / 25 g currants
1 oz / 25 g brown breadcrumbs
large pinch of cinnamon
juice of 2 oranges
bunch watercress

Fill the cavity of the fish with the herbs. Lay them in a shallow, lidded pan, add the water, salt and orange slices, cover them, bring them slowly to the boil and simmer gently for approximately ten minutes or till the fish is cooked. Remove the fish, reserving the liquor. Skin and fillet them (reserving the herbs) and lay them in a warmed serving dish. Melt the butter in a saucepan. Chop together the currants, crumbs and cinnamon, add them to the butter and fry them lightly for a couple of minutes. Remove any woody parts from the herbs which were cooked in the fish, chop them finely and add them to the sauce with the orange juice and approximately half the fish liquor. Cook for a minute then adjust the seasoning to taste if needed. Serve the fish 'garnished' with the green watercress and accompanied by the sauce which should be served separately.

A LOBSTER, PRAWN OR CRAWFISH PATTY

It might surprise most of today's visitors to the Crown Jewels to know that over three hundred years ago they were already a tourist attraction. Not that many of today's visitors could afford a lobster 'patty' as a light snack after their sightseeing. However, seventeenth-century lobsters were relatively cheap and therefore treated with less reverence than today. If you fear to mask the flavour of the lobster by so strong a sauce substitute a light chicken or veal stock for the espagnole sauce.

TO MAKE A LOBSTER PATTY

Patrick Lamb *Royal Cookery* 1710

'Your lobsters being boiled and cut in little peeces take the small claws and the spawn and pound them in a marble mortar; then put to them a ladleful of gravy or broth with a little of the upper crust of a French roll, when it is boiled strain it through a sieve, to the thicknesse of cream and put half of it to your lobsters and save the other half to sauce them with after they are baked, and put to

your lobsters the bigness of an egg of Butter and a little
pepper and salt, squeeze a lemon, put in half a minced
anchovy, warm this over the fire, just as much as melts the
butter; then set it to cool, and sheet your pattypan for a plate
or dish. Then put your lobsters and cover with paste. Bake it
three-quarters of an hour before you want it; then cut your
cover and draw up the other half of your sauce aforesaid with
a little cream, and pour it over your patty, with a little
squeezed lemon juice; cut your cover in 2 and lay it on the
top, 2 inches distant, that they may see what is under. You
may do with crawfish, shrimps, or prawns the same way;
they are all proper for plates or little dishes.'

Recipe Serves 4

8 ozs / 225 g wholemeal pastry
2 ozs / 50 g lobster or crawfish roe, or feeler meat, or prawns
1 oz / 25 g brown breadcrumbs
10 fl oz / 300 ml good espagnole sauce
2 anchovies
juice 1 lemon
1 oz / 25 g butter, melted
12 ozs / 350 g lobster or crawfish meat (cooked) or shelled prawns
freshly ground black pepper

Roll out two-thirds of the pastry, line a pie dish and bake
blind.
Meanwhile to make the sauce put the 2 ozs/50 g of roe, feeler
meat or prawns with the breadcrumbs and the espagnole
sauce in a small pan. Bring to the boil and simmer gently for
15 minutes, then purée it in a food processor or liquidiser.
Keep it warm.
Mash the anchovies and mix with the lemon juice and melted
butter. Mix this into the chosen fish and season with freshly
ground black pepper. Spoon the fish mixture into the flan
case, roll out the rest of the pastry into a fairly thick lid and
place it on the top of the pie. Do not press the lid down as you
will want to remove it. Return the pie to a moderate oven
(375°F/180°C/Gas Mark 5) and bake for 20–25 minutes or
till the lid is well cooked.
Remove the pie from the oven, carefully lift off the lid, and
cut it in half. Pour the sauce into the pie and replace the lid at
an angle so as to display its contents.
Serve warm.

STEAK PIE

In 1660 the mercury thermometer had yet to be invented, let
alone reach the kitchen, so there was no escaping the uncer-
tainties of a wood-fired oven. Perhaps the 'pyes' that poor
Elizabeth burnt at her first try included this early attempt to
get the best out of both the English and French kitchen
worlds.

TO MAKE A STEAKE PYE WITH A FRENCH PUDDYNGE IN THE PYE

The Compleat Cook from *The Queens Closet Opened* 1659

'Season your steaks with Pepper and
Nutmegs, and let it stand an hour in
a tray then take a piece of the leanest
of the legge of mutton and mince it
small with suet and a few sweet
herbs, tops of young time, a branch
of pennyroyal, two or three of red
sage, grated bread, yolks of eggs,
sweet cream, raisins of the sun; work
all together like a Pudding, with
your hand stiff, and roul them round
like balls, and put them into the
steaks in a deep coffin, with a small
piece of sweet Butter; sprinkle a little
verjuice on, bake it, and then cut it
up and roul Sage leaves and fry
them, stick them upright in the
walls, and serve your pye without a
cover, with the juyce of an Orange or
a Lemon.'

46

Recipe   Serves 6

6 small sirloin steaks
salt and freshly ground black pepper
nutmeg
6 ozs /175 g sausagemeat or finely minced lamb
3 ozs / 75 g brown breadcrumbs
1 teaspoon each (1 tablespoon if fresh) dried thyme and parsley
½ teaspoon (½ tablespoon fresh) dried savory
2 ozs / 50 g chopped suet
salt and pepper
2 ozs / 50 g raisins
1 egg, beaten
1 lb / 450 g shortcrust pastry
1 oz / 25 g butter
juice 2 oranges
1 egg, to glaze

Sprinkle the steaks with salt, freshly ground black pepper and nutmeg and set aside.

In a bowl mix the sausagemeat or lamb, breadcrumbs, herbs and suet. Season with salt and pepper, add the raisins and then the beaten egg to bind. Form the mixture into 10–12 small round dumplings and set aside.

Roll out the pastry in one piece so that it will line a pie dish sufficiently large to hold the steaks and dumplings and also fold over the top to make the lid (rather like a Cornish pasty). Line the dish with the pastry, leaving the ends hanging over the side. Put in the steaks and dumplings, dot with the butter and squeeze over the juice of the oranges. Bring up the edges of the pastry and pinch them together, as for a pasty. Brush with the beaten egg. Cook in a moderate oven (375°F/180°C/Gas Mark 5) for 20 minutes, then reduce to 340°F/160°C/Gas Mark 4 for a further 40 minutes or till the pastry is well tanned.

You can leave the pie open as it suggests in the original but I find that it becomes a little dry that way.

BOILED GAMMON

1662 May 19th

'After dinner, Sir W. Penn and his daughter and I and my wife by coach to the Theatre, and there in a box saw *The Little Thief* well done. Thence to Moore fields, and walked and eat some cheese cakes and gammon of Bacon; but when I was come home I was sick, and forced to vomitt it up again. So with my wife walking and singing upon the leades till very late, it being pleasant and mooneshine, and so to bed.'

One wonders whether it was the gammon of bacon or the combination of the bacon with the cheesecakes which had such an unfortunate effect on Pepys's stomach. . . . However, his discomfiture seems to have been very temporary since he felt quite well enough to spend the rest of the evening enjoying the balmy weather on the roof of his house.

There could be little in Giles Rose's 'Gammon of bacon' to upset the stomach although modern tastebuds might be a little more startled by Hannah Wolley's delicious, if bizarre, Bacon Tart on page 63.

FOR A GAMMON OF BACON

Giles Rose *A perfect School of Instruction for the Officers of the Mouth* 1682

'First steep your Gammon in Water and when it is well soked put it a boiling with sage and a good quantity of other Herbs; and when it is boiled raise the skin and stick it with Bays and Rosemary and let it stand to be cold, and then serve it with mustard.'

Recipe   Serves 4

1½ lbs /700 g gammon or bacon joint
2 sprigs each of fresh rosemary, thyme, sage, parsley and 3 bay leaves
wholegrain mustard

Soak the joint for at least one hour in cold water. Discard the water and put the joint in a saucepan, sitting on the sprigs of thyme, sage and parsley. Cover with water, bring to the boil and simmer for 50 minutes. Remove from the water, skin the joint and stick the fat part all over with the sprigs of rosemary and the bay leaves.

Let the joint get totally cold then serve it with wholegrain mustard and fresh brown bread and butter.

SAUSAGES

The combination of 'Raspbury Sack' and sausages sounds thoroughly unappealing yet seventeenth-century recipe books are filled with improbable, yet delicious, combinations. This one obviously had a good effect on Pepys's party so maybe it is worth a try. A little framboise liqueur added to a glass of dry white wine should achieve approximately the right flavour.

TO MAKE SAUSAGES

John Nott *The Cook's Dictionary* 1723

'Having provided Sheeps Guts that are well clean'd, take good Pork, either Leg or Loin, break the Bones small, boil them in just Water enough to cover them; let it be well scumm'd, and season the Liquor with Salt, Pepper, whole Mace, Onion and Shalot; when they have boiled till all the Goodness is out of them, strain the Liquor, and set it by to cool; then mince your meat very small, season it with Salt, Pepper, Cloves and Mace, all beaten; shred a little Spinage to make it look green, and a Handful of Sage and Savoury; add also the Yolks of Eggs and make all the minced Meat and Herbs pretty moist with the Liquor the Bones were boiled in; then roll up some of your minced Meat in Flour, and fry it, to try it if be season'd to your liking; and when it is so, fill your Guts with the Meat. If they are for present spending you may mince a few oysters with your meat.'

Recipe Serves 4

1 lb / 450 g pork belly, skinned and boned with the bones reserved
1 large onion or 4 shallots, peeled and chopped
pinch each salt, pepper and ground mace
2 ozs / 50 g fresh spinach
2 teaspoons of chopped fresh sage or sage and savory mixed or
    2 teaspoons dried mixed sage and savory
2 teaspoons sea salt
1 teaspoon each ground black pepper and ground cloves
½ teaspoon ground mace
2 egg yolks
flour or brown breadcrumbs
2 ozs / 50 g butter

Put the pork bones with the onion or shallots and the pinch of salt, pepper and mace in a small saucepan with water just to cover them. Bring them to the boil and simmer them for 30 minutes, removing the scum as it rises.

Meanwhile mince the pork with the spinach, herbs and spices. Add the egg yolks and then approximately 2 fl oz/60 ml of the stock from the bones. You need just enough to make the mixture reasonably moist.

If you have a sausage skinning machine or if you can persuade your butcher to do it for you, the mixture can now be fed into skins. If however, you decide to do without skins, roll the mixture into sausage or cake shapes. Toss them lightly in flour or in brown breadcrumbs and fry them gently in butter on all sides till cooked through and lightly browned all over. Serve them with pickles or mustard, although they have so much flavour of their own that they scarcely need any help.

51

'BROYLED' LEG, FILLET OR CHOP OF PORK

1667 September 4th

'. . . the business broke off without any end to it, and so I home and thence with my wife and W. Hewer to Bartholomew fayre and there saw *Polichinelli* (where we saw Mrs. Clerke and all her crew); and so to a private house [a quiet tavern] and sent for a side of pig and ate it at an acquaintance of W. Hewer's, where there was some learned Physique and Chymical Bookes; and among others, a natural Herball, very fine.'

A pig was the traditional dish at Bartholomew Fayre, usually roasted, whole, in the open, over a wood fire. Few people today will feel like roasting a whole pig, but Hannah Wolley's recipe comes close to catching the flavour.

In 1667 Pepys was well started on the book collection which was eventually to grow into the library now lodged at Magdalene College, Cambridge, and one can see how his eye immediately lighted on the 'fine' books owned by W. Hewer's friend. Perhaps the herbal was Gerard's, which Pepys later acquired – as did his housekeeper Mary Skinner, whose copy has lately been reunited with Pepys's own in the same library.

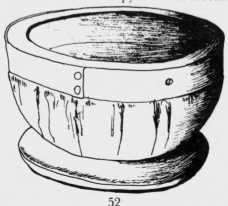

TO BROYL A LEG OF PORK

Hannah Wolley *The Accomplisht Lady's Delight* 1675

'Cut your pork into slices very thin, having first taken off the skinny part of the Fillet, then hack it with the back of your knife, then mince some Thyme and Sage, exceeding small, and mingle it with pepper and salt, and therewith season your collops and then lay them on the Gridiron; when they are enough, make sauce for them with butter, vinegar, Mustard and Sugar and so serve them.'

Recipe   Serves 4

2 lbs / 1 kg pork – either a half leg, sliced in thick 'collops' as Hannah Wolley suggests, or a fillet, sliced thickly, or 4 meaty pork chops
4 teaspoons each fresh thyme and sage, finely chopped. If fresh herbs are not available, use dried but reduce the quantity, especially of the sage
2 teaspoons sea salt
1 teaspoon freshly ground black pepper
2 ozs / 50 g butter
1 oz / 25 g dark brown sugar
2 tablespoons wine or cider vinegar
2 tablespoons wholegrain mustard

Chop and mix well together the herbs, salt and pepper. Coat the meat thoroughly in the mixture on both sides.

On a griddle or a large frying pan, or even under a hot grill, broil the meat rapidly on both sides till it is cooked through and crisply brown on the outside. It will take about three minutes on each side.

Meanwhile in a small pan melt the butter and the sugar, then add the vinegar and mustard and allow all to cook together for a few minutes. Serve the pork immediately, with the sauce in a separate dish.

A LEG OF MUTTON AFTER THE LEGATS WAY

1660 December 2nd

'. . . Mr. Mills made a good sermon; so home to dinner. My wife and I all alone to a leg of mutton, the sawce of which being made sweet, I was angry at it and eat none, but only dined upon the Marrow-bone that we had beside.'

Sweet sauces for roast meats, inherited from the middle ages, still appeared regularly at seventeenth-century meals – even if Pepys did not find them to his taste. However, even he could not have objected to the fruits which decorate la Varenne's excellent dish.

LEG OF MUTTON AFTER THE LEGATS WAY

François de la Varenne *The French Cook* 1653

'After you have chosen it well, beat it well, take off the skin and flesh of the knuckle, whereof you shall cut off the end, lard it with mean lard, flowre it, and pass it in the pan with lard or fresh seam. When you see it very brown, put it in the pot with one spoonful of broth well seasoned with Salt, Pepper, Clove, and a bundle of herbs; you may put in Capers, Mushrooms, Truffles, cover it with a lid closed up with flowre, neither too soft, nor too hard, allayed in water, and seeth it on a few coles the space of three hours. When it is sodden  uncover it; and garnish it with what you have to put it, as Kidneys, Bottoms of Artichokes, sweetbreads, and a short sauce, and about the dish lay out Lemon, or Pomegranate, Barberries and grapes.'

Recipe Serves 6

1 oz / 25 g butter
1 small leg of lamb — approx 4 lbs /2 kg
2 tablespoons flour seasoned with salt, pepper and ground cloves
a bundle of fresh herbs — bay, rosemary, parsley etc
8 ozs / 225 g button mushrooms, cleaned and halved if they are large
1 tablespoon capers, drained and chopped
15 fl oz / 450 ml really well flavoured stock or stock and red wine
  combined
1 oz / 25 g butter
6 lambs kidneys, trimmed and halved
6 ozs /150 g sweetbreads, blanched and sliced
6 artichoke hearts, sliced.
3 ozs / 75 g raspberries, loganberries or redcurrants (fresh/frozen)

Melt the butter till sizzling in a fireproof casserole. Toss the
lamb in the seasoned flour and make sure it is well coated.
Brown the lamb on all sides in the fat till the skin is well
crisped. Tip in any flour that is over, stir well around and
then add the herbs, mushrooms, capers and stock.

Cover the casserole, bring to the boil and then simmer gently
for approximately one hour (15 mins to the pound of lamb).
When the lamb is ready, heat the butter in a shallow pan and
lightly fry the kidneys and sweetbreads till they are just
cooked – the kidneys should still be pink inside. Keep them
warm. In the remains of the butter fry the artichoke heart
slices till they are warmed through then put them to keep
warm with the kidneys.

Warm a serving dish. Carve the lamb and lay it out down the
middle of the serving dish. Arrange the kidneys, sweetbreads
and artichoke hearts around the edge of the dish. Spoon some
of the sauce with some mushrooms over the lamb and put the
rest in a warmed jug to be served separately. Decorate the
lamb with the fruit and serve at once.

STEWED VENISON

1660 January 6th

'This morning Mr. Sheply and I did eat our breakfasts at Mrs. Harpers, my brother John being with me, upon a cold turkey-pie and a goose; from whence I went to my office . . . and I went home and took my wife and went to my Cosen Tho Pepys's and found them just sat down to dinner, which was very good; only the venison pasty was palpable beef, which was not handsome.'

Disguising cheap or even rotten meat in a pie was a favourite trick of the shadier cookshops and it is possible that Cosen Tho had bought in his venison pasty from one such trickster. He might have done better to stick with some stewed venison which was easier to judge before you bought. . . .

TO STEW VENISON

Hannah Wolley *The Accomplisht Lady's Delight* 1675

'If you have much venison and do make many cold Baked meats you may Stew a dish in haste thus; When it is sliced out of your Pye, Pot or Pasty, put it in a stewing dish and set it on a heap of coals with a little claret wine, a sprigg or two of Rosemary, half a dozen cloves, a little grated bread, Sugar, and Vinegar, so let it stew together awhile, then grate on Nutmeg and dish it up.'

Recipe   Serves 4

1 lb / 450 g venison, trimmed and cubed or already cooked and cubed
2 sprigs of rosemary
8 cloves
1 oz / 25 g dark brown sugar
1 oz / 25 g brown breadcrumbs
5 fl oz /150 ml claret
2 fl oz / 60 ml red wine vinegar
salt, pepper and freshly grated nutmeg

Put your venison in a heavy pan or an ovenproof casserole with the rosemary and cloves. Mix the sugar and bread-crumbs into the wine and vinegar and pour over the venison. Bring to the boil and simmer gently for 1¼ hours if it is raw or ½ hour if it is already cooked. Alternatively cook it in a moderate oven (325°F/160°C/Gas Mark 3) for the same amount of time. Adjust the seasoning to taste and grate some fresh nutmeg over the top just before serving.

Like all dark meat dishes the 'stew' is better if it is left for at least 24 hours to 'mature' after it is cooked and before it is eaten.

NEATS' TONGUES

Calves' or neats' tongues are hard to obtain, but with longer cooking the recipe is just as well suited to ox tongue.
Most tongues were eaten cold, as they are today. However la Varenne's recipe is delicious served hot surrounded by its juices. It can then be cooled in them and the remains served cold.

NEATS' TONGUES AND FRESH UDDER IN STOFFADO

François de la Varenne *The French Cook* 1653

'Take your Tongues, and season them with Pepper, Salt and Nutmeg, then lard them with great lard, and steep them all night in Claret-wine, Wine-Vinegar, slic't Nutmegs and Ginger, whole Cloves, beaten Pepper and Salt: let them be put in an earthen pot or pan, covered up close bake them, and serve them up on Pine Molet, or French bread, and the spices over them with some sliced Lemon and Sausages, or without.'

Recipe Serves 8–10

1 ox tongue, trimmed
4 ozs /100 g belly pork or fat bacon cut in thin slices
12 cloves
1 oz / 25 g ginger root (fresh)
½ a whole nutmeg, sliced or 1 teaspoon grated nutmeg
1 teaspoon sea salt
plenty of freshly ground black pepper
5 fl oz /150 ml red wine vinegar
15 fl oz / 450 ml red wine
5 fl oz /150 ml water
slices French bread (optional)
slices of lemon or small sausages (optional)

Fit the tongue into a bowl just big enough for it and cover it
with the pork or bacon. Mix together the cloves, ginger,
spices and seasoning, add the liquids and then pour the
mixture over the tongue. Set aside to marinate for 24 hours.
Move the tongue, and all its bits, into a saucepan/casserole
just big enough to hold it and cover it. Bake for 3–4 hours at
325°F/160°C/Gas Mark 3 or bring it to the boil and simmer
gently for 2 hours.
Remove the tongue from the liquid and skin it carefully.
To serve, slice the tongue and serve it on a dish decorated
with slices of lemon or small, well browned sausages.
Depending on whether you like gravy soaked bread you can
lay your slices of tongue over slices of French bread.

AN OLEO

1669 April 5th

'At noon by appointment comes Mr. Sheres, and he and I to Unthankes, where my wife stays for us in our coach, and Betty Turner with her; and we to the Mulberry-garden, where Sheres is to treat us with a Spanish *Oleo* by a cook of his aquaintance that is there, that was with my Lord in Spain. And without any other company, he did do it, and mighty nobly; and the *Oleo* was endeed a very noble dish, such as I never saw better, or any more of. This, and the discourse he did give us of Spain, and description of the Escuriall was a fine treat.'

As one might gather from la Varenne's comment, his oleo is a simple recipe compared with some. Patrick Lamb's, for example, covers six pages and leaves out nothing in the way of flesh, fowl or vegetable. The dish, which came apparently from the Basque country, became a favourite in Paris as well as London. It seemed to disappear with the Stuarts but survived in Spain not just as a dish but as a phrase – olla podrida – a mish-mash. It tastes much better than that!

AN OLIO AFTER THE SPANISH FASHION

François de la Varenne *The French Cook* 1653

'Take a piece of Bacon, not rusty nor
over fat, a piece of fresh butter, a
pair of Hogs Ears and forefeet, or in
their steed Sheep or Calves feet, a
Rack of Mutton, a Hen, half a dozen
Pigeons, a bundle of Parsley, Leek
and Mint, a clove of Garlick, a little
Pepper, Cloves and Saffron very well
beaten, letting not the quantity of
either exceed, keeping the Saffron
apart till all be ready, a pottle of
hard dry Pease, having been steept
before somewhile in water, with a
pint of boiled Chestnuts. The meat
must not be long boiling, yet the fire
not too fierce, the sauce for your
meat must be as much fine Sugar
beaten small to powder, with as little
Mustard as can be made to drink the
Sugar up.

Where note, I am utterly against
those Olio's into which men put
almost all kind of Roots and Flesh,
especially against putting of Oil, for
it corrupts the Broth, in stead of
adding any goodness thereunto.'

Recipe   Serves 6

6 ozs /160 g dried peas
6 ozs /160 g belly pork or lean green bacon, diced
1 pair pig's ears (if obtainable)
1 pair pig's trotters
3 lamb cutlets, well trimmed
2 pigeons
½ chicken – jointed
1 large handful each of fresh chopped mint and parsley or 2 teaspoons
    each dried mint and parsley
1 large leek, sliced
1 large clove garlic, finely chopped
approx 2 pints /1.2 litres well flavoured beef stock/broth
1 teaspoon each ground cloves and saffron
10 ozs / 300 g cooked chestnuts
4 teaspoons wholegrain or herbed mustard
3 teaspoons sugar
1 teaspoon cornflour

Put the dried peas in a saucepan covered with water, bring to the boil and simmer for 30 minutes or till they are beginning to soften. Drain.

Put all the meats, the herbs, leek and garlic in a flameproof casserole just big enough to hold them. Just cover them with the stock, bring the pot to the boil and simmer for 30 minutes. Mix the spices together and add them, with the peas and the chestnuts to the pot. Continue to simmer gently for a further 45 minutes. Remove the meats and keep aside, cool the juices and when they are cold remove the excess fat from the top.

To serve, return the meats to the pot, bring back to the simmer and simmer for a further 30 minutes before serving. Meanwhile, mix the mustard, sugar and cornflour together in a small pan. Add slowly, 8 fl oz/240 ml of the juices from the pot and cook gently till the sauce thickens; serve it as a relish with the oleo.

BACON TART

A BACON TART

Hannah Wolley *The Accomplisht Lady's Delight* 1675

'Take a quarter of the best Jordan
Almonds and put them in a little
warm water to blanch them, then
beat them together in a mortar with
3 to 4 spoonsfuls of rosewater, then
Sweeten them with fine sugar; then
take Bacon that is clear and white
and hold it upon the point of a knife
against the Fire till it hath dropt a
sufficient quantity, then stir it well
together and put it in the paste and
bake it.'

Recipe   Serves 4

8 ozs / 225 g lean bacon rashers
4 ozs /100 g ground almonds
1½ ozs / 40 g white sugar
2 teaspoons rosewater
6 ozs /175 g wholewheat shortcrust pastry

De-rind and grill the bacon rashers till they are cooked and
just beginning to crisp; remove and chop in largish pieces.
Mix the almonds, sugar and rosewater, then mix in the
bacon. Roll out the pastry and line a 6 inch/15 cm flan case.
Pile in the almond mixture and bake in a moderate oven
(350°F/170°C/Gas Mark 4) for 25 minutes. Eat warm.

CHICKEN WITH COLLIFLOWERS

It would be nice if fanciful to think that Pepys had given his wife a Christmas gift of Robert May's *Accomplisht Cook* which had been published that year, and that she had dipped into it to find an unusual way of cooking their chicken for their Christmas dinner. Had he done so, he would undoubtedly have noted the acquisition in his Diary . . .

TO BOIL A CAPON OR CHICKEN WITH COLLIFLOWERS

Robert May *The Accomplisht Cook* 1660

'Cut off the buds of your flowers and boil them in milk with a little mace till they be very tender; then take the yolks of 2 eggs and strain them with ¼ pint of sack; then take as much thick butter being drawn with a little vinegar and a slict lemon, brew them together; then take the flowers out of the milk, put them to the butter and sack, dish up your capon being tender boiled upon sippets finely carved and pour on the sauce, serve it to the table with a little salt.'

Recipe   Serves 4

1 chicken including giblets
1 onion, peeled and roughly chopped
2 carrots and 1 parsnip or turnip roughly chopped
1 stalk of celery
parsley stalks
6 peppercorns
1 cauliflower
1 pint / 300 ml milk
½ teaspoon mace
3 egg yolks, strained
3 fl oz / 90 ml medium sherry
juice 1 lemon
1 oz / 25 g butter
4 slices wholemeal bread (optional)

Put the chicken in a large pot with its giblets, the onion, carrot, parsnip or turnip, celery, parsley stalks and pepper-corns. Add water just to cover, bring to the boil and simmer gently for 1–1½ hours or till the chicken is really tender and falling off the bones.

Cut the cauliflower in small florets and cook them gently in the milk with the mace added, until they are 'tender'. Drain the cauliflower and keep warm. Reserve the milk.

In a double boiler mix the strained egg yolks with the sherry and lemon juice and heat till it starts to thicken. Then add the butter in small pieces and finally 2 fl oz/60 ml of the juice from the chicken pot and 3 fl oz/90 ml of the cauliflower milk.

Remove the chicken from the pot, drain it and carve it. Lay the chicken pieces out in a serving dish, arrange the cauli-flower florets over the top and spoon the sauce over the cauliflower. Serve at once.

If you wish to serve it as Robert May would, toast 4 slices of wholemeal bread and lay them in the serving dish beneath the chicken.

Use the remains of the chicken meat, the juices from the chicken pot and the milk from the cauliflower to make an excellent soup.

CHICKEN AND LEMON SALAD

1667 July 14th

'Up, and my wife, a little before 4, and to make us ready; and by and by Mrs. Turner came to us by agreement, and she and I stayed talking below while my wife dressed herself; which vexed me that she was so long about it, keeping us till past 5 a-clock before she was ready. She ready, and taking some bottles of wine and beer and some cold Fowle with us into the Coach. . . and so away – a very fine day; and so towards Epsum. . . .'

Elizabeth may well have spent some of the day before preparing some 'cold fowle' according to Joan Cromwell's recipe – if so, let us hope that it put Pepys into a better humour. . . .

A SALLET OF A COLD HEN OR PULLET

The Court and Kitchen of Elizabeth commonly called Joan Cromwell
1664

'Take a hen and roast it, let it be cold, carve up the legs, take the flesh and mince it small, shred a lemmon and a little parsley and onions, an apple, a little pepper, and salt, with oyle and vinegar; garnish the dish with the bones and lemon peel and so serve it.'

Recipe   Serves 6

the meat of a cooked chicken, cut small
the peel and juice of three lemons
1 tart eating apple, cut in small dice (skin on)
1 onion, peeled and finely chopped
2 large handfuls of parsley, roughly chopped
sea salt and freshly ground black pepper
3 tablespoons olive oil

In a bowl mix the chicken, lemon peel, apple, onion and parsley. Sprinkle to taste with sea salt and pepper then add the lemon juice and olive oil and mix well. Blanch the bones by boiling them for 10 minutes in water with a slice of lemon. Clean off any remaining meat or gristle and use them to 'garnish' the dish.

A DISH OF PARTRIDGES

One can only wish that Pepys had been a little more explicit about Captain Cocke's 'dish of partridges' since they obviously lived up to everyone's expectations. Maybe they had been 'Fricacied' like Hannah Wolley's. . . .

TO MAKE A FRICACIE OF PATRIGES

Hannah Wolley *The Accomplisht Lady's Delight* 1675

'After you have Trussed your Partriges, Roast them till they are almost enough, and then cut them to pieces, then having chopped an onion very small fry them therewith, then put to them a half a pint of Gravy, two or three anchovies, a little bread grated, some drawn butter, and the yolks of two or three Eggs beaten up with a little white wine; let it them boyl till they come to be pretty thick and so Dish them up.'

Recipe   Serves 4

2 large partridges, cleaned and trussed
6 rashers fat bacon
10 fl oz / 300 ml espagnole sauce
1 large onion, finely chopped
1 oz / 25 g butter
6 anchovy fillets, very finely chopped
1 oz / 25 g brown breadcrumbs
1 oz / 25g clarified butter
2 egg yolks
5 fl oz /150 ml white wine
salt and pepper

Cover the breasts of the birds with the bacon rashers and roast them in a moderate oven (350°F/170°C/Gas Mark 4) for approximately 35 minutes or till they are all but cooked. Remove them from the oven, pour the juices into the espagnole sauce, and carve the birds into reasonably large pieces of meat. In a wide pan gently fry the onion in the butter till it starts to soften. Then add the pieces of partridge and continue to cook gently for a minute or two. Mix the anchovy fillets with the breadcrumbs, add to the pan, followed by the espagnole sauce and pan juices. Stir well together, bring to the boil and simmer together for 15 minutes. Then add the clarified butter and stir till melted. Mix the egg yolks with the wine, draw the pan off the heat, and add the egg yolk mixture, stir well together and adjust seasoning to taste.
Reheat to serve but do not boil or the egg will curdle.

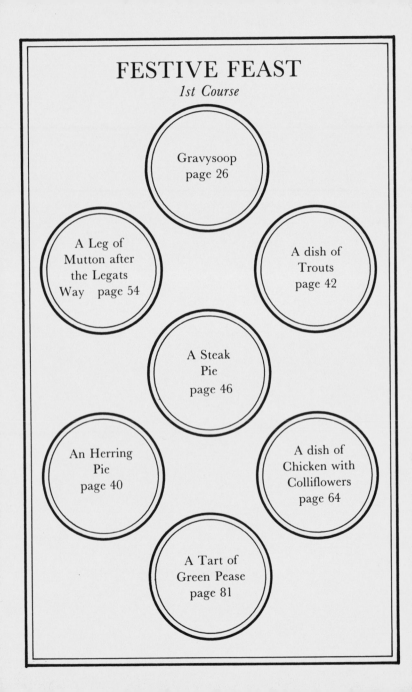

FESTIVE FEAST
1st Course

Gravysoop
page 26

A Leg of
Mutton after
the Legats
Way   page 54

A dish of
Trouts
page 42

A Steak
Pie
page 46

An Herring
Pie
page 40

A dish of
Chicken with
Colliflowers
page 64

A Tart of
Green Pease
page 81

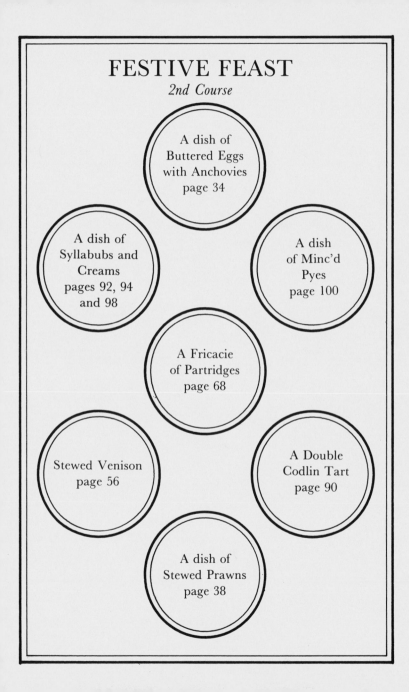

MUSIC

For Pepys, a social occasion that began or ended with food and drink seldom felt complete without music. Usually, the performers were the host and guests, though with advancing wealth and status, invitations to professionals became more common. Pepys's own musicianship commands respect. It included competence – he would not have put it higher than that – on instruments of four different families: viols, violin, flageolet, lute and theorbo (a deeper-voiced cousin of the lute). He loved to sing, and he also composed songs. He was perhaps more proud of this last accomplishment because he had worked at it so hard without ever fully mastering harmony: he had his portrait painted holding his air, 'Beauty, retire', in his hands.

Had the Diary been begun half a century earlier or later, it would have been easier to suggest music appropriate for a Pepys celebration. In 1610, Byrd and Dowland still lived, and gentlemen still expected to be able to hold a part in a madrigal, or to 'touch' a lute. In 1710, Handel arrived in London, and the sound of flute, violin, cello and harpsichord in baroque trio sonatas was already familiar.

Both these styles have been revived and reinterpreted in our own day. But the domestic music made and heard by Pepys and his contemporaries in the 1660s and 1670s is much less clearly defined in our ears, and harder to find on record, or as instrumental parts on a library shelf. As with food and drink, tastes were changing at the time. The sober, gently nasal sound of 'chests of viols' in contrapuntal fantasias was falling out of fashion. Charles II himself preferred to beat time to the less reticent sonorities of newfangled violins in Italianate dances, composed by Lully for the Paris court. The Civil War had not put an end to music-making: as Roger North put it, 'many chose rather to fidle at home, than to goe out, and be knockt on the head abroad.' But it upset the prevailing style and disorganised the music profession. Until the brief career of Purcell (who died in 1695 aged thirty-six) no native genius arose who could marry inherited tradition to the invading continental styles by excelling in both.

So the Restoration period offers relatively unfamiliar music to be explored, not necessarily by professionals. After all, our own musical generation has not only rediscovered pre-classical instruments and sonorities, but trained more young string and wind players than the music profession itself can or should absorb. Offered a modest fee and an appreciative audience, many such would be happy to rehearse and play the consort music of Matthew Locke and William Lawes. It would be fun to reconstruct the informal duets for flageolet (recorder, in effect) and voice that enlivened still summer nights on the 'leads' of Pepys's house in Seething Lane. If there is space, a larger gathering, and a virginals or harpsichord at hand, the more dashing sound of more string players in French or English dance music of the period could be attempted, and the keyboard player could contribute one of the suites written by Purcell or his predecessor John Blow.

As for vocal music, Pepys delighted in the psalms and 'declamatory ayres' of the Lawes brothers (Henry and William), and flattered their style by imitation. But their music is less seductive to our ears than it was to his. This is chiefly because its respect for the sense, metre and, up to a point, the natural pitch intervals of the language ruled out the vocal brilliance which Italian influence later made fashionable. But at least this makes the songs easier for sensitive but untrained voices to sing acceptably. For accompaniment, piano arrangements now sound out of place, and it is still hard to find experienced lutanists. But the guitar, which Pepys heard in London houses more and more often as the 1660s drew on, also provides an appropriate harmonic underpinning for 'Beauty, retire'. (See Richard Luckett's forthcoming edition of the song, obtainable from Magdalene College, Cambridge, where he is Pepys Librarian.)

Lastly, what would nowadays be called 'coarse music' need not be left out of the evening's entertainment. Both in tavern and home, Pepys was used to overhearing or sharing in 'catches', normally written for three unaccompanied voices in canon as a round. In 1667 he bought a copy of John Playford's collection, *Catch that catch can*. The words of many or most catches have been thought unsuitable for mixed company in most ages between his and our own. But their musical invention is often remarkable. Surely Mozart is the only other great composer who could slide as easily as the young Purcell did from sublime melancholy to disreputable wit. Purcell even used what was to be Mozart's favourite G minor key both for his famous four-part Chacony (readily available in string

quartet arrangement) and for this catch, whose verbal inde-
licacies are shared out between the voices like the pieces of a
musical jigsaw.

A Catch

by Mr. H. Purcell

1 Once, Twice, Thrice, I Ju - lia try'd, the
scorn - - ful Puss as__ oft de - nied, and

2 since, and since I can__ no bet - ter, bet - ter
thrive, I'll crin - - ge to ne' er a bitch a - live, so kiss my Ar-

3 so kiss my Ar-, so kiss my Ar-, so kiss my Ar-,dis-dain-ful
Sow, good Cla - ret, good Cla - ret is__ my__ Mist - ress__ now.

DRINKS

1633 October 29th

'Many were the tables, but none in the Hall but the Mayors and the Lords of the privy Councell that had napkins or knives – which was very strange. We went into the Buttry and there stayed and talked, and then went into the hall again; and there wine was offered and they drunk, I only drinking some Hypocras, which doth not break my vowe, it being, to the best of my present judgement, only a mixed compound drink, and not any wine – if I am mistaken, God forgive me; but I hope and do not think I am not.'

Some of the wines and other drinks mentioned in the Diary, and therefore suitable for a Pepys party, are discussed in the Introduction (page 19). Traditional recipes abound for making them more palatable or exciting. Present-day taste is unlikely to fancy many of the caudles and possets – rich and sweet melanges of ale with butter, cream, or eggs – that warmed winter evenings in chilly seventeenth-century houses; besides, such treatments assumed unhopped ale, not the bitter beer of our own time. Most people anyway will have their own preferred party drinks, simple or compound. But 'burnt' claret, the hypocras with which Pepys allowed himself to be deceived, and Christmas lamb's wool – spiced ale with apples – are simple devices that have changed little over the centuries. Party guests who have followed Pepys's intermittent example and sworn off wine altogether may be glad too of a cup which could certainly have been made from summer fruit available to Pepys, whether or not the idea occurred to him.

AN HYPOCRAS OF WHITE WINE

Giles Rose

'Take about three quarters of the best white wine, a pound and a half of sugar, an ounce of cinamon, two or three leaves of marjoram, 2 grains of whole pepper; let all this pass through your bag, with a grain of musk, 2 or 3 slices of Lemon, when it hath stood and infused altogether for the space of 3 to 4 hours. That of claret may be made the same way.'

Mulled wine

Into an enamelled or stainless steel pan put 3 bruised cloves, ½ stick of cinnamon, lemon and orange peel pared, 4 ozs of sugar, and half a pint of water. Boil together for 15 minutes; then add grated nutmeg, a pint of full-blooded red wine, and a wine-glass of port. Do not allow to boil again, but heat, strain, and serve.

Hypocras

Bruise together a cinnamon stick, ½ oz coriander seeds, a blade of mace, and 1 oz of green ginger. Boil a quart of water with 8 ozs sugar for 5 minutes to make syrup.

Macerate the spices for an hour or two in some of the wine (red or white) you propose to use. Heat the mixture with the rest of the bottle of wine, the juice of half a lemon, a gill of brandy, and syrup to taste; strain clear and serve.

Lamb's wool

Roast 8 apples; mash them, and add a quart of old ale (Winter Warmer or equivalent will do nicely). Press and strain; add grated nutmeg, powdered ginger, and sugar to taste as it heats.

Mixed fruit cup

Mash together half a pound of strawberries, half a pound of raspberries and half a pound of red currants. Add to them a breakfastcupful of sugar, and the juice of 2 lemons.

Pour over them as much boiling water as is required, and leave it for 12 hours. Strain; decorate with whole strawberries and verbena.

(A recipe from Mrs C.F. Leyel's
Summer Drinks and Winter Cordials)

Samuel Pepys of Brampton in Hunting
tonshire Esq: Secretary of y Admiralty to
his Ma:ty King Charles y Second: Descended
of y antient family of Pepys of Cottenham in Cambridg

ROOTES AND GREENSTUFFS

Apart from noting the arrival of this season's new peas, or the occasional purchase of some 'sparrow grass' in the market, Pepys seldom mentions vegetables or 'herbes' in the Diary. This would suggest that he was not a great vegetable lover but we know, from other contemporary writers, that a huge variety of vegetables and fruits were available in London. Even if her husband was not too keen on them Elizabeth is bound to have bought and used at least some vegetables as they were much cheaper than meat.

To illustrate what these might have been I have temporarily ignored the Diary and given a selection of vegetable dishes that Pepys's friends, such as John Evelyn, were cooking and eating during the 1660s.

Printed for Righ: Lownes

BUTTERED RICE

TO BOYLE RICE

The Closet of the eminently learned Sir Kenelme Digby Kt., opened 1669

'The manner of boiling rice to eat with Butter is this. In a pipkin pour upon it as much water as will swim a good finger's breadth over it. Boil it gently till it be tender, and all the water drunk into the rice; which may be a quarter of an hour or less. Stir it often with a wooden spoon or spatule that it burn not to the bottom; but break it not. When it is enough pour it in a dish and stew it with some butter and season it with sugar and cinnamon. This rice is to appear dry excepting for the butter which is melted in it.'

Recipe Serves 4

8 ozs / 225 g brown rice
water just to cover it in the pan
2 ozs / 50 g butter
½ teaspoon cinnamon
1 teaspoon dark brown sugar
sea salt (optional)

Put the rice in a pan and just cover it with water. Bring it to the boil and simmer it gently till the rice is cooked and the water absorbed. You may need to add a little more water along the way.

Add the butter, cinnamon and dark brown sugar and stir till the rice is well coated with all three. If you prefer a more savoury flavour, reduce the quantity of sugar slightly and add sea salt to taste.

Serve hot as a vegetable.

PARSNIP SALAD

PARSNEPS

John Evelyn *Acetaria* 1699

'Parsnep, Pastinaca, Carrot; first boil'd, being cold, is of itself a Winter-Sallett, eaten with Oyl, Vinegar and etc and having something of Spicy, is by some thought more nourishing than the Turnep.'

Recipe   Serves 4

2 lbs /1 kg young parsnips, well scrubbed and sliced in rounds approx
    ½ inch /1 cm thick
sea salt
freshly ground black pepper
2 tablespoons wine vinegar
4 tablespoons olive oil

Steam or boil the parsnips until tender and then drain. While they are still warm, lay them out on a dish and sprinkle them liberally with sea salt and freshly ground black pepper. Mix together the vinegar and olive oil, spoon over the parsnips and leave to get cold. Serve cold as a salad but not chilled.

GREEN PEA PIE

A TART OF GREEN PEASE

Hannah Wolley *The Accomplisht Lady's Delight* 1675

'Boyl your pease tender, and pour them out into a Cullender, season them with Saffron, Salt, sweet butter and Sugar, then close it and let it bake almost an hour, then draw it forth and Ice it, put in a little verjuice and shake it well, then scrape on sugar and so serve it.'

RECIPE   Serves 4

8 ozs / 225 g wholemeal shortcrust pastry
1 lb / 450 g fresh or frozen green peas
2 ozs /50 g butter
1½ ozs / 40 g dark brown sugar
a good pinch of powdered saffron
1 small teaspoon of sea salt
2 fl oz / 60 ml cider vinegar

Roll out two-thirds of the pastry and line an 8 inch/20 cm flan dish. Bake it blind. If they are fresh boil the peas briskly for 5 minutes or till they are cooked; if they are frozen, thaw and drain them. Melt the butter in a pan, add the sugar, saffron and salt and then the peas; mix them well together. Pile the peas into the flan case and top with the remains of the pastry leaving a hole in the lid.

Bake for 25 minutes in a moderate oven (350°F/170°C/Gas Mark 4). Remove the pie from the oven and add the vinegar through the hole. If you wish it to have a genuine seventeenth-century flavour, sprinkle some sugar over the top and return it to the oven for five minutes to 'ice' it before serving it hot.

SWEET POTATO PUDDING

A GOOD POTATOE PUDDING, YE BEST

The Receipt Book of Mrs. Ann Blencowe 1694

'Take one pound of potatoes, boyl'd
and peeled and cold mash them
through a strainer. Then add one
pound of fresh butter, melted, 10
eggs, half a pound of sugar, half a
nutmeg, slic't; mix these together
and put it in a quick oven. One hour
will bake it.'

Recipe   Serves 4

1 lb / 500 g sweet potatoes, cooked and mashed
4 ozs /100 g butter
½ teaspoon grated nutmeg
1 oz / 25 g dark brown sugar
salt and pepper
4 eggs

Mix the butter, nutmeg, sugar, salt and pepper into the
potatoes and ensure that they are well blended. Whisk the
eggs together with a fork and add them to the mixture. Spoon
it into an ovenproof dish and bake, uncovered in a moderate
oven (350°F/170°C/Gas Mark 4) for 35 minutes or till it is
slightly risen and browned on top.

The original proportion of butter to potato would make a richer dish
than most people could cope with today.

SPINACH CONDIMENT

SPINACH CONDIMENT TO ACCOMPANY ALL SORTS OF BOILED FLESH

John Evelyn *Acetaria* 1699

'Spinach, Spinachia: of old not us'd in Sallets, and the oftener kept out the better; I speak of the crude; But being boil'd to a Pult and without other water than its own moisture, is an most excellent condiment with Butter, Vinegar or Limon, for almost all sorts of boile'd Flesh, and may accompany a Sick Man's Diet. 'Tis laxitive and Emollient and therefore profitable for the Aged, and (though by original a Spaniard) may be had at almost any Season and in all places.'

Recipe

8 ozs / 225 g fresh spinach, washed and finely chopped
juice of 2 oranges
1 tablespoon cider or wine vinegar
1 oz / 25 g butter

Put the spinach in a pan with the orange juice and vinegar and cook gently for 15–20 minutes until the spinach is cooked almost to a puree (or a 'pult'). Add the butter, stir well and season to taste if required. Serve either warm or cold with the meat.

NB. This is sufficient for 4 people 'as a condiment'. If you want to use it as a vegetable you will need to triple the quantities.

ROAST TURNIPS

TURNEPS ROAST IN PAPER WITH BUTTER AND SUGAR

John Evelyn *Acetaria* 1699

'Some roast Turneps in a Paper
under the Embers, and eat them
with Sugar and Butter.'

Recipe

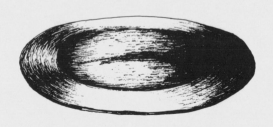

1 turnip per person
approx ½ oz /10 g butter per person
½ teaspoon dark brown sugar per person
aluminium foil

Peel the turnips and gouge a hollow out of the top of each.
Cut out squares of silver foil big enough to wrap each turnip
loosely and rub them well with butter.
Stuff the hollow in the top of each turnip with a bit of butter
and ½ teaspoon of dark brown sugar pressed well down.
Wrap them loosely in the foil and bake them in a moderate
oven (350°F/170°C/Gas Mark 4) for approximately 45 minutes or till they are cooked.

A SALAD

A SALLETT

Robert May *The Accomplisht Cook* 1660

'The youngest and smallest leaves of
spinage, the smallest also of sorrel,
well washed currants, and red beets
round the centre being finely carved,
oyl and vinegar and the dish
garnished with lemons and beets.'

Recipe   Serves 4

*8 ozs / 225 g fresh, young spinach leaves, trimmed, washed and well
dried*
*4 ozs /100 g fresh young sorrel leaves, trimmed, washed and well dried.
If they are not obtainable, substitute watercress*
*2 ozs / 50 g currants, plumped and washed in boiling water, then
drained*
8 ozs / 225 g cooked beetroot, peeled
1 lemon
sea salt
4 tablespoons olive oil
2 tablespoons wine vinegar

Mix together the spinach and sorrel or watercress leaves and
toss them with the currants. Slice the beetroots, making fancy
patterns with a knife or biscuit cutter. Arrange the tossed
leaves and currants on an open bowl or a dish and arrange
some of the beetroot in a pattern in the middle. Slice the
lemon and blanch it briefly in boiling water. Arrange the rest
of the beetroot with the sliced lemon in a pattern around the
outside of the dish. Sprinkle with sea salt. Mix together the
oil and vinegar and spoon over the salad just before serving.

A GRAND SALAD

ANOTHER GRAND SALLET

Robert May *The Accomplisht Cook* 1660

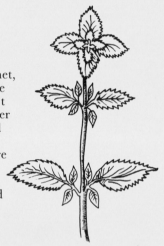

'All sorts of good herbs, and little
leaves or red sage, the smallest
leaves of sorrel, and the leaves of
parsley pickt very small, the
youngest and smallest leaves of
spinach, some leaves of salad burnet,
the smallest leaves of lettuce, white
endive and charvel, all finely pick't
and washed and swung in a strainer
of a clean napkin and well drained
from water: then dish it in a clean
scowered dish and about the centre
capers, currants, olives, lemons
carved and slict, boiled beetroot
carved and slic't and dished round
also with good oyl and vinegar.'

Recipe Serves 6

2 cabbage lettuce hearts, washed and well dried
4 ozs /100 g young spinach leaves, washed and well dried
2 ozs / 50 g young sorrel or watercress leaves, washed and well dried
a small handful of parsley, washed and de-stemmed
if possible, a teaspoonful each of fresh young sage leaves, salad burnet
*   and chervil. A little fresh mint can also be included. These herbs*
*   should be roughly chopped*
2 heads endive, the leaves broken off at the base and kept whole
1 oz / 25 g currants, plumped and drained
2 ozs / 50 g black olives, stoned
1 oz / 25 g capers
4 ozs /100 g boiled fresh beetroot, peeled
2 lemons, sliced and the slices blanched briefly in boiling water
6 tablespoons olive oil
2 tablespoons wine vinegar

Toss together the lettuce, spinach, sorrel or watercress, parsley and herbs. Arrange the leaves of endive round the outside of a dish or bowl to form a bed – their tips all pointing outwards from the centre of the bowl. Pile the leaves in the middle and flatten them out. Arrange the currants, olives, capers, beetroot and lemon slices in patterns on top of the leaves – as formally as possible. Just before serving, mix together the oil and vinegar and spoon over the salad.

APPLE FRITTERS

Fritters or 'fritours' in early English cooking usually refer to
pancakes – the traditional Shrove Tuesday dish – but by
Pepys's time the word was also acquiring its more modern
sense of a batter coating for a fruit or savoury morsel of some
kind. In Mrs. Blencowe's recipe the batter can be used either
way – to coat apples as she does, or slightly thinned down, as
a pancake mix.

FRITTERS

The Receipt Book of Mrs. Ann Blencowe 1694

'Take 11 eggs and 9 of ye yolks, beat
them well and putt to them a pint of
Cream. Mix it with ye finest flower
about ye thickness of a pudding and
put to it salt, Nutmeg, Mace and
Cinnamond a pretty deal and beat it
well together and let it stand 3 or 4
hours before you fry them, cover'd
up before the fire. Then pare 18
small pipins and slice them as thin as
a Wafer. When you are ready to fry
them add to your butter, sack
brandy, strong Ale or beer, not
bitter, of each 5 spoonfulls mixt
together and made scalding hot.

Then put it into ye stif bater and
beat it well together. Let there be in
ye stew pan 2 pound of beef dripping
and 2 pound of hogs Lard. When it
boyles well up dip your slices into ye
batter and put them quick into ye fat
and another must stand to turn and
take them out, laying them on a hot
coarse Cloth before ye fire till you
have nough to send up. You will
scarse complain of this quantity
being too small, but 'tis just as it was
given me. . .'

Recipe Serves 4

3 egg yolks
a good pinch each of ground nutmeg, mace and cinnamon
2 ozs / 50 g sieved flour, white or wholemeal
5 fl oz /150 ml double cream
2 small or 1 large cooking apple
3 fl oz / 90 ml of sweet sherry
clean, light oil to deep fry

In a mixer beat the egg yolks with the spices, then add the
flour and cream alternately till you have a smooth batter.
Set aside to rest for at least 30 minutes.
Peel and thinly slice the apple. Add the sherry to the batter
and beat it well. Heat the oil and when it is almost smoking,
dip the slices of apple in the batter and fry them carefully.
They should take 2–3 minutes each. When they are done
drain them on kitchen paper and keep them warm till all
the fritters are ready. Serve them hot either alone or with
whipped or 'churned' cream.
For pancakes, thin the batter slightly with water and make as
normal.

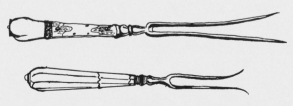

JOAN CROMWELL'S DOUBLE TART

1663 July 27th

'. . . meeting Creede . . . he and I over the water to
Fox-hall [Vauxhall]. . . . And then to the new
Spring garden, walking up and down; but things
being dear and little attendance to be had, we went
away, leaving much brave company there. And so to
a less house hard by, where we liked very well their
Codlin tarts (having not time, as we entended, to
stay the getting ready a dish of peese); and there
came to us an idle boy to show us some tumbling
tricks, which he did very well and the greatest bend-
ing of his body that ever I observed in my life.'

It is amusing to note that even three hundred years ago the
smartest eating house was not necessarily the best – let alone
the cheapest. If the codlin tarts Pepys and Mr. Creede
sampled at the 'less house' were anything like Joan Cromwell's Double Tart, they would have been unlikely to do as
well at the Spring Garden, even if they had been able to get
served.

TO MAKE A DOUBLE TART

The Court and Kitchen of Elizabeth commonly called Joan Cromwell
1664

'Take some codlings tenderly boyled
and peel them, cut them in half, fill
your tart, put in a quarter of a 100
codlings, 1½ pounds of sugar, a few
cloves and a little cinnamon, close
up the coffin and bake it; when it
comes out of the oven take a quart of
cream, 6 eggs, a quatern of sugar
and a sliced nutmeg, beat all these

well together, pour them into the tart and set your tart in the oven for 8 minutes, when it comes out cut off the lid and having a lid cut in flowers ready, lay it on and garnish it with preserves of damsons, raspberries, apricots and cherries and place a preserved quince in the middle and strew it with sugar biskets.'

Recipe   Serves 6

6 ozs /175 g wholemeal or mixed wholemeal and white flour
3 ozs / 75 g butter
1½–2 lbs / 750 g—1 kg Bramley cooking apples peeled, cored and thickly
*   sliced, or small Cox's pippins halved and cored*
2 ozs / 50 g sugar
8 cloves
½ teaspoon cinnamon
7 fl oz / 200 ml double cream
2 egg yolks
1 oz / 25 g sugar
½ teaspoon freshly grated (if possible) nutmeg
preserved damsons, cherries or fresh/frozen raspberries

Make some shortcrust pastry with the flour and butter and line a 8–10 inch/20–25 cm flan dish. Bake blind. Arrange the apple slices in the pie, sprinkle over the sugar, cloves and cinnamon, cover with foil and cook for 20 minutes in a moderate oven – 350°F/170°C/Gas Mark 4.

Mix together the cream, egg yolks, sugar and nutmeg and when the apples in the pie are just cooked remove the foil and pour in the cream mixture. Return to the oven, lower the temperature to 300°F/150°C/Gas Mark 2 and continue to cook for a further 20 minutes or till the custard is set.

Remove from the oven and decorate with the damsons, cherries or raspberries 'strewn liberally'. Serve either warm or cold.

CREAM TOASTS

The constant references in the Diary to eating 'a dish of
cream' would lead one to suppose that Pepys and Lady Slany
really did share a passion for eating cream or drinking cream
with slices of brown bread. . . . Even though seventeenth-
century cream was thinner than our own, few twentieth-
century stomachs could handle so rich a dish. A toasted
version such as Patrick Lamb's Cream Toasts makes an
excellent alternative. . . .

TO MAKE CREAM TOASTS

Patrick Lamb *Royal Cookery* 1710

'Take two French rolls or more
according to the bigness of your dish,
and cut them in thick slices, as thick
as your finger, crumb and crust, lay
them on a silver or brass dish, put to
them a pint of cream, ½ pint of milk,
strew over them beaten cinnamon
and sugar, turn them frequently till
they are tender soaked, so as you can
turn them without breaking; so take
them with a slice or skimmer for

your cream; break 4 or 5 raw eggs,
turn your slices of bread in the eggs
and fry them in clarified butter;
make them of a good brown colour,
not black; take care of burning them
in frying; scrape a little sugar round
them, have a care you make them
not too sweet. You may well serve
them hot for a 2nd course, being well
drained from your butter in which
you fryed them; but they are most
proper for a plate of a little dish for
supper.'

Recipe Serves 4

4 slices good brown bread
5 fl oz /150 ml double cream
2 fl oz / 60 ml milk
1 oz / 25 g sugar
large pinch of cinnamon
1 egg
½ oz /15 g clarified butter
dark brown sugar

Mix together the cream, milk, sugar and cinnamon and pour
it over the slices of bread laid out in a flat dish. Make sure
they are well covered and leave to soak for 10 minutes. Beat
the egg on a plate. Heat the butter in a frying pan till almost
sizzling. Take each slice of bread out of the cream and dip it
thoroughly on both sides in the egg, then fry it gently in the
butter till it is well browned, but not blackened on each side.
Take it out and drain it for a minute on kitchen paper. Serve
at once well sprinkled with dark brown sugar.

CHURNED CREAM

1667 July 1st

'Up betimes about 4 a-clock, waked by a damned noise between a sow gelder and a cow and a dog, nobody after we were up being able to tell us what it was. After being ready, we took coach; and being very sleepy, drouzed most part of the way to gravesend; and there light and down to the new Battery which are like to be very fine... Then informed ourselfs where we might have some Creame, and they guided us to one Goody Best's, a little out of the town towards London-road; and thither we went with the Coach and find it a mighty clean, plain house, and had a dish of very good cream to our liking; and so away presently, very merry, and fell to reading of the several *Advices to a Painter* which made us good sport. . . .'

The 'dish of cream' that Goody Best served Pepys and his party had probably been 'churned' such as the one in John Nott's recipe. If you do not share their fondness for it on its own, it is delicious with a fruit salad, tart or pie. If you wanted to treat your cream a little more exotically you would find it hard to better Patrick Lamb's recipe for 'Fry'd creame'.

TO MAKE CHURN'D CREAM

John Nott's *The Cook's Dictionary* 1723

'Take two Quarts of thick Cream,
put to it four Spoonfuls of Rosewater
and a quarter of a pound of fine
Sugar, put it into a Churn and churn
it; as the Froth rises, take it off, and
put it into a Dish, and serve it.'

Recipe   Serves 4

5 fl oz /150 ml double cream
½ oz /15 g castor sugar
1 tablespoonful orange flower or rosewater
birch or balloon whisk

Put the cream, sugar and rose or orange water into a deep jug
and whisk with the birch or balloon whisk by briskly rubbing
the whisk between one's hands to turn it backwards and
forwards in the cream. This creates more of a 'froth' than
whisking by the conventional methods, although if neither
are available whisk the cream in the normal way. The cream
can be eaten alone with a sweet biscuit or used wherever
crème chantilly is called for. The orange-flower version with
strawberries is delicious.

CHEESECAKE

1669 April 25th

'Abroad with my wife in the afternoon to the park –
where very much company, and the weather very
pleasant. I carried my wife to the Lodge, the first
time this year, and there in our coach eat a cheesecake and drank a tankard of milk. I showed her this
day also first the Prince of Tuscany, who was in the
park – and many very fine ladies. And so home, and
after supper to bed.'

The cheesecake served at 'the Lodge' might well have been
similar to the one Joan Cromwell recommends in her book
which had been published five years earlier.

TO MAKE CHEESECAKES THE BEST WAY

The Court and Kitchen of Elizabeth commonly called Joan Cromwell
1664

'Take two gallons of new milk and
put into it 2 spoonfuls and a half of
runnet, heat the milk a little less
than blood warm, cover it close with
a cloth until you see the cheese be
gathered, then with a scumming dish
gently take out the whey, so when
you have drained the curd as clean
as you can, put the curd in a sieve
and let it drain very well there; then
to two quarts of curd take 1 quart of
thick cream, 1 pound of butter, 12
eggs, 1½ pounds of currants, and
with cloves, nutmeg and mace
beaten, ½ pound of good sugar, ¼
pint of rosewater, so mingle it well
together and put it in puff paste.'

96

Recipe   Serves 4

4 ozs /100 g soft curd or cream cheese (If you feel energetic make your own. Otherwise a good 'bought' cream cheese will do quite well, but taste before you buy, sometimes it is too salt for sweet uses)
2 fl oz / 60 ml double cream
½ oz /10 g unsalted butter, softened
1 egg
1 oz / 25 g washed currants
a pinch each of ground cloves, nutmeg and mace
1 oz / 25 g sugar – dark brown gives a good flavour but does colour the cheesecake
1 teaspoonful rosewater
the juice of a small lemon (If you are using a tart curd cheese you will not need the lemon but most cream cheeses are rather bland so benefit from a little sharpening up)
8 ozs / 225 g puff pastry
1 teaspoon granulated sugar

Mix well together the cheese, cream, butter, egg, currants, spices, sugar, rosewater and lemon juice. Roll out two-thirds of the pastry and line a shallow pie dish or 'plate pie' dish. Spoon in the cheesecake mix. Cover with the remaining pastry and sprinkle the top with the granulated sugar. Bake for 30 minutes in a moderately hot oven (375°F/180°C/Gas Mark 5) or till the pastry is cooked and lightly tanned. Serve warm or cold.

SYLLABUB

Twentieth-century syllabubs are wine-based desserts; in the
seventeenth century they were whisked and flavoured cream
drinks – not unlike a milk shake. Although wine was often
used as a base any fruit juice with a definite flavour of its own
would do as well.

A SULLABUB

The Closet of the eminently learned Sir Kenelme Digby, Kt., opened
1669

'Take a reasonable quantity (about
half a porringer full) of the syrup
that hath served in the making of
dried plums; and into a large
sullabub pot milk or squirt or let fall
from high, a sufficient quantity of
milk or cream. This syrup is very
quick of the fruit and very weak of
sugar and therefore makes the
sullabub exceedingly well tasted.
You may also used the syrup from
drying cherries.'

98

Recipe

*5 fl oz /150 ml well flavoured juice from stewing plums, rhubarb,
   blackberries, blackcurrants, or cherries*
5 fl oz /150 ml double or whipping cream

When you stew the fruit ensure that the juice is strong and
not too sweet. Each fruit will require a different amount of
sweetening but as a general rule 1 tablespoon dark brown
sugar or honey, the juice of 1 lemon, 2 tablespoons of water
and approx 2 lbs of fruit will give approximately ½ pint of
well flavoured juice. If it is too tart add a little more sugar
when it is cooked. Cool the juice. Put the juice in a tall jug
and pour in the cream. With a birch or balloon whisk, whip
the mixture till it is very frothy and slightly thickened. Pour
into glasses and drink.

99

MINCE PIES

1662 December 25th

'The sermon done, a good Anthemne fallowed, with vialls . . . but I stayed not . . . but walked home again with great pleasure; and there dined by my wife's bedside with great content, having a mess of brave plum-porridge and a roasted Pullet for dinner; and I sent for a mince-pie abroad, my wife not being well to make any herself yet. After dinner sat talking a good while with her. . . .

December 26th

Up. My wife to the making for Christmas-pies all day, being now pretty well again. . . .'

Mince pies are almost the only one of our Christmas dishes which were as regularly eaten in Pepys's time as today. Even though a seventeenth-century mince pie still contained the meat which had originally been predominant, the balance of the recipe had already shifted towards the sweet ingredients. You have to concentrate quite hard to taste the difference between Mrs. Blencowe's and our own.

TO MAKE MINC'D PYES

The Receipt Book of Mrs. Ann Blencowe 1694

'Take a large Neat's tongue and Boyle it till it will peel. When peeled cut all that is fitt for use into thin slices, weight it and take half as much more fresh beef suitt; shred your meat small and mix your suet with it; mix both together as small as possible; put to it a pound of raisins of ye sun, ston'd, five hard pippins, ye rind of a lemman and ye Rind of a sevil orange shred very small. Shred too your Raisins and pippens

amongst ye meat. Mix all this well
together and put into them two
nutmegs, some sinemone, mace and
a few cloves all finly beaten, a
quarter of a pint of sack, a little salt
and three quarters of a pound of
suger, some Canded Cylon Lemon
and oringe peel cut into thin slices,
three pounds of courants cleen
pick't, wash't and dry'd and ye Juce
of four Lemons.'

Recipe   Makes 12

4 ozs /100 g tongue, ham or other cooked meat, chopped small
2 ozs / 50 g beef suet
1 tart eating apple, peeled and finely chopped
4 ozs /100 g each raisins and currants
4 ozs /100 g candied peel
3 ozs / 75 g dark brown sugar
rind and juice of 1 lemon and 1 orange
1 teaspoon each cinnamon and nutmeg (ground)
½ teaspoon each mace and cloves (ground)
5 fl oz /150 ml brandy
8 ozs / 225 g wholemeal shortcrust pastry

Mix the meat, suet, apple, raisins, currants, peel and sugar
well together. Grate in the rind of the fruit. Mix the spices in
the fruit juices and the brandy and mix well into the dry
ingredients.
Set aside to mature for at least 24 hours.
Roll out the pastry and line a 10 inch/25 cm shallow pie dish,
or individual patty pans. Fill with the mincemeat and cover
with pastry lids. Slit them and brush with egg if you like a
shiny lid. Cook in a moderately hot oven (375°F/180°C/Gas
Mark 5) for approximately 20 minutes or till the pastry is
done. Serve hot or cold.

GINGERBREAD

Mrs. Blencowe's gingerbread has no raising agent and so is quite solid when it is cooked. It could well be stored and cut into small lozenges like 'chocolatte'. Alternatively it can be buttered and eaten like ordinary bread.

GINGERBREAD

The Receipt Book of Mrs. Ann Blencowe 1694

'Take 3 quarters of a pound of sugar, an ounce and half of Ginger, half an ounce of Cinamon in fine pouder. Mingle all these with your flower, and make it up with 3 pound of Treacle, just so stiff as will keep it from running about ye board; then put in 3 quarters of a pound of Melted butter, and stirring it well together; then strow in some more flower by degrees, enough to make it so stif as will make it up in cakes. The oven must be no hotter than for manchets, lett it stand in ye Oven 3 quarters of an hour; wash out the treacle with 2 or 3 spoonfuls of Milk, bake it on buttered papers; mince in also 2 ounces of Oringe pill, and preserved sittern 2 ounces, and 2 great nuttmegs grated.'

•

Recipe

1 lb plain flour
½ oz /15 g ground ginger
pinch each cinnamon and nutmeg
4 ozs /100 g dark brown sugar
1 oz / 25 g candied peel
4 ozs /100 g butter softened
1 lb / 450 g black treacle

Sift the flour and the spices in the bowl of an electric mixer.
Add the sugar and peel, then the softened butter and the
treacle. Beat hard until the ingredients form a stiff paste.
Press this into a 10 inch/25 cm greased loaf tin. Bake in a
moderate oven (350°F/170°C/Gas Mark 4) for 45 minutes.
Remove and cool on a rack. Eat with butter.

CURRANT CAKE

1661 January 7th

'To the office; and after that to dinner, where my brother Tom came and dined with me; and after dinner (leaveing 12d with my servants to buy a cake with at night, this day being kept as Twelfe day), Tom and I and my wife to the Theatre and there saw *The Silent Woman* ... an excellent play.... From thence by link to my Cosen Stradwickes.... And after a good supper we have an excellent cake, where the mark for the Queene was cut; and so there was two queenes, my wife and Mrs. Ward; and the King being lost, they chose the Doctor to be King, so we made him send for some wine....'

Seventeenth-century Christmas celebrations centred not on Christmas day but on Twelfth Night (January 6th, unless the 6th fell on a Sunday when celebrations were held on the 7th). It was traditional to bake a rich Twelfth Night cake in which would be buried a dried pea and a dried bean. When the cake was cut the lady who got the pea in her slice would be queen for the night and the gentleman who got the bean would be king. However, on this occasion the pea got cut in half as the cake was cut – so they had to have two queens. Thos Stradwick was a provision merchant in Snow Hill – hence the excellence of his cake!

TO MAKE AN EXTRAORDINARY GOOD CAKE

Robert May *The Accomplisht Cook* 1660

'Take half a bushel of the best flour you can get, very finely searced, and lay it on a large pastry board, make a hole in the middle thereof, put to it three pounds of the best butter you can get; with 14 pounds of currants finely picked and rubbed, three quarts of good new thick cream, warmed, 2 pounds of fine sugar beaten, 3 pints of new ale barm or yeast, 4 ounces of cinnamon beaten fine and searsed, also an ounce of beaten ginger, 2 ounces of nutmegs beaten fine and searsed; put in all these materials together, and work  them up into indifferent stiff paste, keep it warm till the oven be hot, them make it up and bake it, being baked an hour and a half ice it, then take 4 pounds of double refined sugar, beat it and searce it and put it in a clean scowered skillet the quantity of a gallon, and boil it to a candy height with a little rosewater, then draw the cake, run it all over and set it in the oven till it be candied.'

Recipe

1 lb / 450 g wholemeal flour
3 ozs / 75 g butter
1½ ozs / 40 g sugar
½ oz /10 g each of ground cinnamon and ginger
¾ oz / 20 g ground nutmeg
12 ozs / 325 g currants
2 teaspoons bicarbonate of soda
20 fl oz / 600 ml double cream
8 ozs / 225 g granulated sugar
2 tablespoons rosewater

Rub the butter into the flour as for pastry, then add the sugar, spices and currants together. Mix well. Heat the bicarbonate in a little of the cream then add it, with the rest of the cream, to the other ingredients and mix it well. It will make a very dry paste. Spoon or press the mixture into an 8 inch/20 cm cake tin with a removable base and bake in a moderate oven (350°F/170°C/Gas Mark 4) for 1¼ hours. Test with a skewer to make sure it is ready, then cool slightly on a rack. Turn it right way up and place on an ovenproof dish.

In a flat pan slowly melt the sugar with the rosewater and boil it for a few minutes till the sugar is melted and bubbling fiercely, then pour/spoon it over the top of the cake.

If it crystallises, either add a little water to it when it will normally come back, or use it in its crystalline form – this is opaque and rather attractive.

Return the cake to a low oven (330°F/150°C/Gas Mark 2) for 15 minutes to 'candy' the icing.

JOHN NOTT'S BISKETS

1664 March 18th

'So to my brother's, and to the church and with the gravemaker chose a place for my brother to lie in, just under my mother's pew. But to see how a man's tombes are at the mercy of such a fellow, that for 6d he would (as his own words were) "I will justle them together but I will make room for him" – speaking of the fullness of the middle Isle where he was to lie. . . .

. . . . At noon my wife, though in pain, comes; but I being forced to go home, she went back with me – where I dressed myself and so did Besse; and so to my brother's again – whither though invited as the custom is at about 1 or 2 a-clock, they came not till 4 or 5. But at last, one after another they came – many more than I bid; and my reckoning that I bid 120, but I believe there was nearer 150. Their service was six biscuits apiece and what they pleased of burnt claret – my Cosen Joyce Norton kept the wine and cakes above – and did give them out to them that served, who had white gloves given them.'

Pepys goes on to say how grateful he was to 'Mrs. Holden' who had organised the funeral party and, no doubt, the baking of the biscuits that the guests consumed in such quantities. The following recipes come from John Nott's *Cook's Dictionary*, a compendium of recipes from the previous half century that he published in 1723. The Nun's biscuits on page 112 in particular would have been very suitable for a funeral. . . .

TO MAKE BISKETS

John Nott *The Cook's Dictionary* 1723

'Take eight eggs, a little Rose water, some Sack, and a pound of fine Sugar; beat them together for an Hour; then put in a Pound of Flour and half an Ounce of Coriander seeds; then beat them well together, butter your Pans and put in your Batter, and set it into the Oven for half an Hour; then turn them brush them over the Top with a little of the Eggs and Sugar that you must leave out at first for the Purpose, and set them in again for a quarter of an hour.'

Recipe   Makes 24

2 eggs
4 ozs /100 g sugar
1 teaspoon rosewater
2 fl oz / 60 ml medium sweet sherry or madeira
4 ozs /100 g flour, white or wholemeal
¼ oz / 5 g coriander seeds crushed

In an electric mixer beat the eggs, sugar, rosewater and sherry or madeira for 4–5 minutes.
Reserve 1 tablespoonful of the mixture. Gradually beat in the flour and the coriander seeds. Spoon the mixture into well greased and floured mince pie or 'patty' tins and bake in a moderate oven (325°F/160°C/Gas Mark 3) for 15 minutes. Remove and brush with the remains of the egg and sugar mixture. Return to the oven for a further 15 minutes. Remove from the tin and cool on a rack.

COMFITS OF ORANGE RIND

1669 March 9th

'. . . by and by away, and with my Wife and Bab.
and Betty Pepys and W. Hewers . . . to my Cosen
Stradwicks. . . . And I was glad of this opportunity
of seeing them, they being good and substantial
people, and kind. And here met my cousin Rogr, and
his wife and my cousin Turner; and here, which I
never did before, I drank a glass, of a pint I believe,
at one draught, of the juice of Oranges of whose peel
they make comfits; and here they drink the juice as
wine, with sugar, and it is a very fine drink; but it
being new, I was doubtful whether it might not do
me hurt.'

Three years earlier, when no one was looking, Pepys had
pulled an orange off a tree in Lord Brooke's garden in Hack-
ney, to see what the English-grown fruit tasted like. The
craze for drinking orange juice must have been slower to
catch on if this was the first time he had tried drinking it.
Comfits or candied fruit and fruit peel had been around for
a long time. In the same year that Pepys drank his juice
this recipe for 'candying' was published in *The Closet of the
eminently learned Sir Kenelme Digby Kt., opened* 1669.

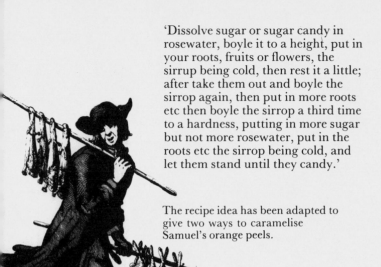

'Dissolve sugar or sugar candy in rosewater, boyle it to a height, put in your roots, fruits or flowers, the sirrup being cold, then rest it a little; after take them out and boyle the sirrop again, then put in more roots etc then boyle the sirrop a third time to a hardness, putting in more sugar but not more rosewater, put in the roots etc the sirrop being cold, and let them stand until they candy.'

The recipe idea has been adapted to give two ways to caramelise Samuel's orange peels.

Recipes

1. With a vegetable peeler, peel the rind off 3 oranges in very thin strips. Cut them into matchsticks and boil them for 10 minutes in water. Toss them in some sugar and put them in an ovenproof dish in a moderate oven (350°F/170°C/Gas Mark 4) for 15–20 minutes or till they are crisp and caramelised. Cool.

2. With a sharp knife or a vegetable peeler, peel the rinds from 3 oranges. Cut the peel into matchsticks and boil it in water for 10 minutes. Melt approx 4 tablespoons of sugar in a pan and as soon as it starts to caramelise add the orange rind. With tongs, move the rinds around in the caramel till they are thoroughly coated and the caramel has stopped sizzling and is darkening further. Remove them with tongs and allow them to dry on a rack.

'MARMALADE' OF QUINCES OR OTHER FRUIT

1663 November 2nd

'. . . Creed and I to the Coffee-house and then to the Change; and so home and carried a barrel of oysters with us, and so to dinner; and after a good dinner left Mrs. Hunt and my wife making Marmalett of Quinces. . . .'

November 4th

'Home to dinner and very pleasant with my wife, who is this day also herself making of Marmalett of Quince, which she now doth very well herself.'

Preserve making has always been catching and Elizabeth was obviously eager to try her hand with the quinces after her session with Mrs. Hunt. A seventeenth-century 'marmalett' or marmalade could be made from any fruit which was boiled and crushed with sugar to help preserve it; the exclusive link between marmalade and oranges is of comparatively recent origin.

COTIGNACS AND MARMALADE OF QUINCES

Giles Rose *A perfect School of Instruction for the Officers of the Mouth* 1682

'Take what fruit you please, cut it in quarters and boyl it; and when it is boyled let the water run well from it, then strain it through a collender or Hair Strainer, then boyl half a pound of sugar a Soufle and being boiled, put into it a pound of your Marmalad, first taking it from the fire, and let it stand till it be cold, and when it is cold dress or fashion it upon a plate and mark it as you do other pastes. This may serve to make a Tart either laced or covered.'

Recipe

1 lb / 450 g quinces, pears, apples or other hard fruit
8 ozs / 225 g sugar

Peel the fruit, quarter or slice it roughly, put it in a saucepan just covered with water, bring to the boil and simmer till it is well cooked. Drain the fruit, then purée it either in a food processor or through a sieve. Drain the fruit very well once it is pureed. In a wide pan melt the sugar and allow it to cook until it is just beginning to turn colour. Remove it from the heat immediately and add the fruit purée to it. Stir the mixture well and allow it to cool. It may then be 'shaped' and eaten alone or used as a filling for a fruit tart or pie.

NUN'S BISKETS

THE NUNS BISKET

John Nott *The Cook's Dictionary* 1723

'Take the Whites of twelve Eggs and
beat them to a Froth, a Pound of
Almonds, blanch them and beat
them with the Froth of the Whites of
Eggs, as it rises; then take the Yolks
and two Pound of fine Sugar and
beat them all together; then mix the
Almonds with the Sugar and Eggs;
then add half a Pound of flour with
the Peel of four Lemons grated, and
some citron shred small; put the
Composition in little Cake Pans and
bake them in a quick Oven and,
when they are coloured, turn them
onto Tins to harden the Bottoms;
and before you set them in the oven
again sift on them some double
refined sugar. Let the Pans be
butter'd and fill them but half.'

Recipe Makes approx 24

3 eggs separated
4 ozs /100 g ground almonds
6 ozs /160 g sugar
4 ozs /100 g white or wholemeal flour
grated peel of 2 lemons

Whisk the egg whites till just holding their shape then beat in
the ground almonds. Whisk the egg yolks with the sugar till
pale and ribbony, then mix the two mixtures together. Add
the flour and the lemon rind and mix all well. Spoon the
mixture onto a well greased baking tin – a large teaspoonful
should be enough for each biscuit. Sprinkle the biscuits with
sugar and bake them in a moderate oven (325°F/160°C/Gas
Mark 3) for 40 minutes. Remove from the tin and cool on a
rack.

CHECK-LIST OF COOKERY WRITERS AND BOOKS

Dates given are for the actual, or if in brackets conjectural, year of first printing. However, in a few cases recipes have been taken from subsequent editions. Most of the titles are seldom found outside the British Library and other specialist collections. References are therefore given to modern editions or facsimiles where these exist.

Ann Blencowe	*The Receipt Book of Mrs. Ann Blencowe* 1694 This family household book survived in a private collection and was first published in 1925.
Joseph Cooper	*The Art of Cookery* 1654 Cooper is described in his book as 'chiefe Cook to the late King'. Authorship would have been the natural consequence of losing his situation, as happened after 1789 to the cooks whose employers lost their heads in the French Revolution.
Elizabeth (Joan) Cromwell	*The Court and Kitchen of Elizabeth commonly called Joan Cromwell* 1664 After the Restoration, Royalist propagandists tried hard to present Puritan figures as yokels and killjoys as well as regicides. This book was part of the campaign, but it only succeeded in showing that the Lord Protector's widow was as fond of cooking as her husband had been of music. Paperback edition, 1983, by Cambridgeshire Libraries, Broadway, Peterborough.

Kenelme Digby	*The Closet of the eminently learned Sir Kenelme Digby Kt., opened* 1669 As scholar, epicure, privateer, and husband of Venetia Stanley, Kenelme Digby (1603–1665) lived a full, perhaps over-full, life. His recipes – more of them for drinks than for food – were published posthumously by his sons, whom he had unkindly omitted from his will.
John Evelyn	*Acetaria, a Discourse of Sallets* 1699 See Introduction, page 9. Facsimile edition by Prospect Books, 1982.
Patrick Lamb	*Royal Cookery* 1710 Lamb was appointed to Charles II's kitchen in 1662, as 'youngest child of pastry'. He became 'First Master Cook' in 1688, the year of the Glorious Revolution, and went on to serve Queen Anne until his death in 1709, so represents an entire era of royal (and extravagant) cookery.
François de la Varenne	*The French Cook* 1653 See Introduction, page 14. A recent edition of the French original, *Le Cuisinier françois*, introduced and edited by Jean-Louis Flandrin and Philip and Mary Hyman, is distributed by Prospect Books.
Gervase Markham	*The English Hus-wife* 1615 The author of this, the second volume of his *Country Contentments*, has been called 'the earliest hackney writer' – and he was also active in the horse trade. His recipes were reprinted throughout the century.

Robert May	*The Accomplisht Cook* 1660 See Introduction, page 14.
John Nott	*The Cook's and Confectioner's Dictionary* 1723 Encyclopaedic length and alphabetical arrangement made this book by the Duke of Bolton's cook popular for many years. It took recipes from 'the most celebrated Artists; and also the nicest and most curious Dames and House-wives our Country has produced'. But Nott also saw to it that 'France, Italy, Spain, Germany and other Countries' were represented. Facsimile edition by Lawrence Divington 1980.
William Rabisha	*The Whole Body of Cookery Dissected* 1661 See Introduction, page 14.
Giles Rose	*A perfect School of Instruction for the Officers of the Mouth* 1682 The title sounds less awkward in the French original (1662): *L'école parfaite des officiers de Bouche.*
Hannah Wolley	*The Accomplisht Lady's Delight* 1675 First published in 1675 this book went into many subsequent editions. The first edition contained instructions for preserving and candying, 'physick & chirurgery' and 'angling' as well as cookery. The recipes are relatively simple and well laid out. Subsequent editions were revised and enlarged. The recipes in the book were taken from the 2nd edition published in 1677.

Books of uncertain authorship

The Compleat Cook 1659
This often-reprinted book originally formed part of an earlier three-volume work, *The Queens Closet Opened*, by 'W.M.', 1655. Facsimile edition by Prospect Books, 1984.

The Family Dictionary 1695
Attributed to 'J.H.', this book's title prefigures John Nott's more substantial publication a generation later (q.v.).

The Gentlewoman's Cabinet Unlocked (1664)
This and the item that follows are both in the Pepys Library, bound up with other small books and pamphlets. It is incorrectly dated to c.1680 in the index to the Companion volume of the main edition of the Diary. The author designed it for 'Gentlemens Houses', with some stress upon 'Pancakes, Fritters, Tansies, Puddings, Custards, Cheesecakes, And such like fine Knacks'.

The Gentlewoman's Delight in Cookery (n.d.)
'All young Gentlewomen and Servant-Maids' will find this book 'very beneficial', according to the author, whose description of it covers the whole title-page. Though short, the volume would have seemed adequate to most kitchens at the time; besides, 'I conceived it not amiss to Collect such Curiosities as are not vulgarly known; the which . . . must, in all probability, Redound to the Advantage and Accomplishment of either Sex.' (Also see Introduction, page 13.)

Further bibliographical details about these and other cookery of the period may be found in Laura B Axford, *English Language Cookbooks, 1600 to 1973* (Detroit, 1976); Katherine G. Bitting, *Gastronomic Bibliography* (1939; then Ann Arbor, 1971; London 1981); and A.W. Oxford, *English Cookery Books to 1850* (1913 and 1977).

ENGLISH/AMERICAN TERMS

Almonds: flaked .... sliced
        ground........................... powdered – either
                                                  bought that way or
                                                  done in a processor

Apples – cooking (Bramleys).......... English cooking apples
                                                  are tarter than any
                                                  American ones. Use the
                                                  sharpest eating apples
                                                  to be found

Bacon: rashers............................... slices
       green .... unsmoked

Butter: 4 ozs/100 g......................... 1 stick

Cream: double.............................. heavy. Substitute very
                                                  well chilled whipping
                                                  cream if not available
       whipping........................... whipping

Dripping .... lard

Flour – plain .... all purpose
       wholemeal .... wholewheat

Leeks – onion family .... if not available
  shaped like overgrown   substitute shallots.
  scallion...................................... One average leek
                                                  weighs approx 8 ozs

Lamb cutlets .... substitute lamb chops

Loganberries................................. substitute raspberries

Mustard and cress .... substitute watercress

Partridges .... if not available
                                                  substitute Cornish hens

Pigeons .... if not available
                                                  substitute squab

Pigs trotters.................................. pigs feet

Quinces .... substitute crab apples

Rosewater .... scented water usually
                                                  obtainable in
                                                  pharmacies

Silverside .... large joint from rump of beef suitable for long slow cooking

Sorrel... substitute watercress

Suet .... if not available substitute with two-thirds the quantity of lard or butter

Treacle (black)................................ molasses

Wholemeal – bread etc .... wholewheat bread etc

CONVERSION TABLE

Liquid Measure

Imperial	Metric	American
1 fl.	30 ml	$1/8$ cup
2 fl	60 ml	$1/4$ cup
4 fl	120 ml	$1/2$ cup
5 fl/$1/4$ pt	150 ml	$2/3$ cup
6 fl	175 ml	$3/4$ cup
7 fl/$1/3$ pt	200 ml	$7/8$ cup
8 fl	250 ml	1 cup
10 fl/$1/2$ pt	300 ml	$1\frac{1}{4}$ cups
12 fl	350 ml	$1\frac{1}{2}$ cup
14 fl	400 ml	$1\frac{3}{4}$ cup
15 fl/$3/4$ pt	450 ml	2 cups
18 fl	500 ml	$2\frac{1}{4}$ cups

20 fl/1 pt	600 ml	2½ cups
1¼ pts	750 ml	3 cups
1½ pts	900 ml	3¾ cups
1¾ pts	1 l.	4¼ cups
2 pts	1.2 l.	5 cups
2¼ pts	1.25 l.	5¾ cups
2½ pts	1.5 l.	6¼ cups
2¾ pts	1.6 l.	7 cups
3 pts	1.75 l.	7½ cups